Embracing Calm: Meditation Journeys for Inner Peace

Anne E. Beall, PhD

Embracing Calm: Meditation Stories for Inner Peace
Copyright © 2024 by Anne Beall/Beall Research, Inc.

Cover Designed by Atiq Ahmed

All images generated using 123rf.com

ISBN: 979-8-985888485 (Paperback)
ISBN: 979-8-985888492 (Hardcover)

Other Books by Anne E. Beall

Cinderella Didn't Live Happily Ever After: The Hidden Messages in Fairy Tales

Only Prince Charming Gets to Break the Rules: Gender and Rule Violation in Fairy Tales and Life

Heroic, Helpful & Caring Cats: Felines Who Make a Difference

Heartfelt Connections: How Animals and People Help One Another

Community Cats: A Journey Into the World of Feral Cats

Strategic Market Research: A Guide to Conducting Research that Drives Businesses

"Imagination will often carry us to worlds that never were. But without it, we go nowhere."

—Carl Sagan

To Judi, for her unwavering encouragement in my writing journey and her steadfast belief in my words.

Contents

Preface

Have you ever longed for a sanctuary, a place where daily life fades into the background? In our fast-paced world, we often crave a moment to pause, let go of our stresses, and simply be.

Imagine finding peace. Perhaps you've experienced this feeling while on vacation or in the quiet of nature. That sense of stepping away from the endless chatter of your thoughts, even if just briefly. Physically escaping to a tranquil setting like a quiet mountaintop or a secluded rose garden isn't always possible, but what if you could travel there in your mind?

This is the essence of meditation journeys. They offer a way to experience these peaceful moments without leaving your home. You're starting an internal voyage, guided towards relaxation and the discovery of serene landscapes within your own mind.

Unlike traditional meditation, where you observe your breath, which can be challenging, these are guided journeys where you become the main character in each story. Picture yourself taking a leisurely stroll along a pristine beach, embarking on an exploration of a majestic waterfall, or visiting an enchanting royal castle.

You can immerse yourself in these stories simply by reading them, or let the audiobook guide you through each journey. The goal is to offer an escape from incessant thoughts, providing relief from worries and life's pressures. Such escapes are crucial for mental well-being. We all need time away in whatever form we can take it.

I originally wrote these journeys during the pandemic to aid those confined to their homes, offering a way to escape the chaos of life. After receiving heartwarming feedback from readers who expressed their appreciation for their relaxing qualities, I've expanded them to provide a more immersive experience. Each journey has been expanded and is now longer, enabling a deeper state of relaxation.

So, I invite you to step into each journey. Allow yourself the gift of time to breathe, and within these pages, discover a haven for your mind. Welcome to your inner calm.

—Anne E. Beall

How to Use this Book

These meditation journeys are designed to be immersive, enabling you to escape into a haven of tranquility. By engaging in another world, you can detach from your thoughts and emotions, landing in a realm where worries and troubles are left behind.

So, slow down, take a deep breath, and allow yourself to be fully present on these journeys. Let them transport you to a place of calm and clarity, where you can find solace and rejuvenation.

Each chapter is a standalone experience, offering a unique meditation journey for you to explore. Here are some tips on how to make the most of your experience.

1. Find a Quiet Space: Set aside some time in a quiet and comfortable environment where you won't be disturbed. This will enable you to focus on the journey without distractions.

2. Get Comfortable: Find a comfortable seating position or lie down if you prefer. Make sure your body is relaxed and supported, allowing you to let go and fully enjoy the experience.

3. Breathe Deeply: Begin by taking a few deep breaths to center yourself and calm your mind. Focus on the sensation of the breath as it enters and leaves your body, allowing yourself to relax more deeply with each exhale.

4. Visualize: Use the image at the beginning of each chapter to guide your imagination and to visualize each journey. Alternatively, for those who are naturally imaginative, allow your mind to wander freely, allowing the imagery to come to life in your mind.

5. Take Your Time: There's no rush—take your time to fully experience each meditation journey. Pause whenever you feel the need to soak in the sensations or reflect on your experience.

6. Enjoy the Journey: Most importantly, enjoy it! Allow yourself to be fully present and open to each journey. Each one offers an opportunity for you to experience feelings of peacefulness, wonder, and contentment.

By incorporating these tips into your practice, you'll be able to make the most of each meditation journey, finding peace and relaxation amidst the chaos of life. Take your time, breathe deeply, and enjoy each journey ahead.

Journey 1: Lighthouse

Inhale slowly, counting to three. Exhale gently, counting to three, releasing any tension. Repeat this process, taking three deep, purposeful breaths. With each exhale, allow your body to relax more deeply.

Imagine you rent a bright green kayak at a small harbor nestled off the vast ocean. With a gentle push, you glide into the open water. Feel your paddle cutting through the ocean, propelling you forward. On your right is the coast, a picturesque scene of small white homes with black shutters, sitting elegantly at the edges of cliffs. Their quaint beauty adds to the charm of the landscape. You pause to admire the coast.

The calm ocean sparkles under the bright sun, its surface reflecting shades of sapphire. Looking up, you see the sky, a clear and expansive vista of serene blue meeting the waters off in the horizon. Three seagulls soar gracefully overhead. Listen to their calls, transported through the air in a light breeze that brushes your face. Breathe in the fresh, salty scent.

You feel the gentle waves beneath your kayak as you paddle along. Occasional pieces of driftwood float past, each piece a silent storyteller of journeys unknown. The rhythmic motion of paddling, the resistance of the water against your arms and shoulders, brings a sense of connection to the natural world. It's a peaceful experience, where each stroke propels you further along the stunning coastline. Tall green fir trees stand guard behind scrubby brush perched on boulders that lead to rocky shores.

Your journey leads to a series of small inlets, each with a tiny sandy beach, a hidden gem along the coast. One inlet, with a secluded beach and a shallow cave, catches your eye. Intrigued, you paddle into the calm waters and step out onto the shore. Your water shoes protect your feet from the pebbles and rocks. The sandy beach in front of the shallow cave seems like a nice place to sit.

You enjoy the view of the waves rolling in and out, each leaving its mark on the rocky sand. Each wave is different: some push further up the shore, while others barely reach where the last one stopped.

In the distance stands a lighthouse, a solitary structure on a rugged outcrop in the ocean. The afternoon sun bathes the landscape in a warm glow, perfect for your next adventure. You get into your kayak and paddle towards the lighthouse. Feel your arms pushing you across the water, invigorated by the movement.

The lighthouse's abandoned state is noticeable, with a large, faded red stripe wrapping around the top and the rest of the structure covered in peeling white paint, hinting at a neglect that time has only deepened. Pulling your kayak onto the beach, you discover a pathway leading to higher ground. As you hike through the tall beach grass, swaying in the gentle breeze, a sense of solitude surrounds you—it's as if this place has been forgotten by time.

You traverse the pathway to the lighthouse, where you pull open the creaky outer door. Its resistance is a testament to its long abandonment. You call out, "hello?" but receive no answer. The spiral staircase inside beckons, and you ascend, holding onto the smooth metal rail that winds up to the top. Your footsteps are the only sounds you hear as you climb. At the top, the view is breathtaking—a vast expanse of ocean, the serene beach, and your little green kayak below. Imagine days gone by when this lighthouse was a beacon of hope, guiding ships safely through fog and darkness.

Descending the stairs, you return along the pathway to your kayak. The tide has brought an assortment of wooden debris to the shore. Among the driftwood, an old green bottle catches your eye. Its surface is opaque. It likely once had a cork stopper, now long gone. You touch the smooth, cold surface, wondering what it once held.

As you get into your kayak, you look back at the lighthouse. To your surprise, a light flickers from its top. The sight is both eerie and mesmerizing—a hidden secret of the abandoned lighthouse coming to life. Let this mysterious image linger in your mind.

The rhythm of your paddling syncs with the gentle lapping of the waves against your kayak, creating a meditative cadence. As you glide through the water, a group of dolphins catches your eye, playfully swimming in the distance. Their graceful movements and joyful leaps weave a spell of magic and wonder. One by one, they arc through the air. Together, they dive in and out of the water with effortless elegance. Watching them, you're swept up in their aquatic ballet. Eventually, they swim towards the horizon, their departure a poignant reminder of the ocean's many inhabitants.

The vastness of the water unfolds before you, an infinite mosaic of blues and greens. In one corner, a deep emerald green. In another, a soothing aquamarine. Dark navy gradually gives way to a lighter blue, capturing every hue that lies in between. This expanse is more than a mere spectacle of color—it's a living, breathing world teeming with life, shrouded in mysteries, and whispering secrets, stretching endlessly in every direction.

As you gaze at the clear waters beneath your kayak, a gray fish catches your eye. It's about the size of your hand, with a slender, streamlined body that cuts effortlessly through the water. Its scales shimmer, blending with the ocean's colors. The fish moves with purpose, its tail flicking side to side in swift, smooth motions. For a moment, it hovers near the surface, before it darts away into the depths, leaving only ripples behind.

It's time to paddle back to the harbor. As you arrive at the dock, you feel a sense of accomplishment and joy. You step out of the kayak, taking one last look at the ocean. Its vastness reminds you of the endless possibilities and mysteries that life holds.

Now it's time to leave your kayak and come back to your current environment. Take this feeling of peace and wonder into your day or evening.

Journey 2: Luxury Rail Trip

Inhale slowly, counting to three, filling your lungs with air. Exhale gently, counting to three, releasing any tension. Repeat this process, taking three deep, purposeful breaths, allowing your body to relax more deeply with each one.

Envision stepping back into a bygone era, where train travel symbolized the pinnacle of elegance. Your adventure begins with your arrival at the station, ready to embark on a journey aboard a luxurious train. The station buzzes with the energy of passengers and staff. Porters in crisp white gloves and rich burgundy uniforms move gracefully, taking your luggage with respectful nods. They guide you to your private cabin, navigating through hallways that boast thick red carpets, walls with deep wood paneling, and windows and doors accented with polished brass fixtures that gleam under the soft lighting. A subtle fragrance fills the air in the hall—a blend of polished wood with a hint of lemon from the freshly cleaned surfaces.

When you enter your cabin, you are impressed by the rich, deep mahogany walls, accented with elegant maple inlays, which create a welcoming and cozy atmosphere. The bed, covered in a sumptuous burgundy spread and topped with soft, plush pillows, promises a night of restful sleep and luxurious comfort. Nearby, an overstuffed chair with a velvety surface, positioned close to a reading lamp, invites you to read or unwind during your journey. You touch the fabrics in the room and inhale the subtle scent of polished wood.

The adjacent bathroom, though compact, reflects the opulence of the era with a dark green marble sink and shower. Across from the bed, a beautiful wooden desk beckons you to sit and capture your thoughts. You unpack and settle into your new accommodations.

As the train leaves the station, you gaze through the window, observing the many buildings and the people strolling on the sidewalks. The train gently sways as it moves. You enjoy this rhythmic and comforting movement.

After relaxing in your room, you venture out to explore the train. The dining car, a testament to refined elegance, welcomes you with tables dressed in immaculate white tablecloths, bearing exquisite china. Crystal ware, catching the rays of the setting sun, scatters rainbows of light across the room.

You head to the next compartment, which is the lounge car. Furnished with antique chairs upholstered in forest green leather, you can imagine relaxing here in the evening. The slight fragrance of fine spirits fills the air. Seats are thoughtfully arranged in groups and along panoramic windows, offering splendid views of the passing scenery. Polished wooden tables dot the space, perfect for resting a drink or a book. Ambient lighting casts a warm glow, enhancing the refined atmosphere. You inhale the scents of aged beverages and rich leather.

Next is the observation car, a masterpiece with its glass ceiling and sidewalls. You sink into one of the deep purple swivel chairs and immerse yourself in the passing scenery. The transition to the serene countryside unfolds before you. Meadows and pastures change to a small town and then to a lush forest. The beautiful scenery and rhythmic clatter of the train over the tracks is soothing.

As dusk falls, you return to the dining car, now aglow with soft candlelight. The china, adorned with a delicate bird motif, adds to the elegant setting. Impeccably dressed servers in burgundy uniforms attend to your every need.

After dinner, the observation car beckons. The night sky is breathtaking. Stars twinkle like distant jewels against the velvety darkness. As you gaze upwards, you imagine connecting the stars with lines and see a variety of shapes, including an arrow and the outline of an animal. In this moment, under the vast sky, you feel a profound sense of connection to the universe as you move through this world, seeing stars that are millions of miles away.

The gentle murmur of fellow passengers softly fades into the background. Soothing rhythms of the train lull you into a deeper state of relaxation. The soft clatter of the wheels on the tracks, the occasional distant whistle, and the rhythmic sway of the train are tremendously pleasant.

Eventually, you take a leisurely stroll through the train. The lamp-lit corridors cast a warm, golden glow. In the lounge car, you pass people who are talking and laughing together in small groups. Their joy at being together is palpable. You pass by windows framing snapshots of the passing countryside—rolling hills, tranquil rivers, and sleepy towns.

Making your way back to your cabin, the plush red carpet feels soft under your feet, adding to the sense of serenity. Retiring to your bed, you leave the curtains open, allowing the moon's silver light to fill your room. When you settle in, the train's gentle movement and the cozy pillows surround you with comforting tranquility. You drift into sleep, your mind wandering through the memories of the day.

The following morning, you awaken to the first light of dawn. The train has traveled through the night and the early sun peeks through your window. As you rise, you feel refreshed and peaceful, ready to embrace the day.

This morning you discover more of the train's treasures. The library compartment, with its shelves of leather-bound books and overstuffed navy chairs by the windows, is a splendid retreat. Shelves brimming with thousands of books stretch up to the ceiling. You browse the extensive collection, which ranges from classics to mysteries, romance novels, and non-fiction works about travel around the world. Settling in, you spend the morning engrossed in reading. Feel the book in your lap and the plush chair cradling your back. Outside, the beautiful landscape unfolds—forests, rivers, and distant mountains pass by.

In the afternoon, the train gently snakes its way through the picturesque valleys nestled between majestic snow-capped mountains. As you peer out the window, the train delves into a lush forest, where the long branches of trees seem to extend their welcoming arms, brushing against the passing train. Emerging from this woodland, you're greeted by a serene clearing, where a small river glimmers under the sunlight. The river cascades over rocky formations, forming frothy rapids that leave white caps in their wake.

The train makes its way into a deep gorge, its walls rising steeply. You're captivated by the immense scale of the rugged, deep brown cliffs that soar on both sides. A thought crosses your mind. Were dynamite blasts used to carve the tracks through this imposing terrain? The gorge echoes with the rumble of the train's passage, creating a sound that reverberates through the canyon walls.

As evening approaches, you visit the observation car, watching the sunset over the distant mountains. The sky is ablaze with orange and deep yellow colors that seem to have been painted across the sky with a gigantic paintbrush. The fading sunlight casts a golden glow on everything it touches, including the fields outside the window. Shadows lengthen, and the mountains' silhouettes become more pronounced against the fiery sky. The other passengers marvel at this breathtaking view.

Now it's time to leave this luxury train. Come back to your present environment and take these feelings of wonder and peacefulness into your day or evening.

Journey 3: Ancient Forest

Inhale slowly, counting to three, feeling the air expand your lungs. Exhale gently, counting to three, releasing any tension in your body. Take three deep, purposeful breaths, letting each exhalation relax you more deeply.

Imagine standing at the edge of an ancient forest at the break of dawn. The sky blooms in gentle shades of pink and orange. The air is fresh and cool. As you step onto the forest path, a carpet of green moss cushions your feet. The forest seems to welcome you.

Touching the bark of a gigantic tree, you look up into the pink sky, feeling lucky to be in this place.

You walk along a path that meanders through the heart of the forest. The trees stand tall and majestic, forming a diverse tapestry of ancient oaks, towering maples, and graceful beech trees. Their branches intertwine, creating a lush canopy, while their robust trunks reflect centuries of growth and resilience. Their leaves rustle gently in the morning breeze, creating relaxing sounds. The sunlight filters through the trees, creating patterns of light and shadow that dance on the forest floor. You breathe deeply, filling your lungs with the earthy scent of the woods.

As you go deeper into the forest, the birdsong grows louder. Red robins, blue jays, and small wrens serenade you with their songs, each distinct yet in harmony. The rustling and scurrying of chipmunks and squirrels add to the chorus. Now and then, a branch snaps when you walk on it. These sounds from nature have a calming effect on you.

Further along, you hear sounds of water and eventually come across a babbling brook to the right of the path. Its crystal-clear waters cascade over smooth stones, creating a gentle, gurgling sound. You approach the brook and sit on a nearby rock. Dip your hands into the cool water, feeling it surround your fingers. Watch as the sunlight sparkles on the surface. Listen to the water's murmur— a timeless sound that speaks of the earth's natural rhythms. Let the sound of the water ground you in the present moment.

Continuing your journey, you encounter an ancient oak tree, its presence commanding yet welcoming. This grand sentinel of the forest, with its enormous trunk, gnarled bark, and sprawling branches, has stood watch for over 400 years. You sit under its protective canopy with your back against the sturdy trunk. Feel a connection to its strength and wisdom. This tree has seen countless sunrises and sunsets, weathered storms, and basked in sunlight, a testament to its endurance. Imagine its roots, deep and strong, anchoring it to the earth. Visualize yourself drawing strength from this connection as you sit against the trunk beneath its sprawling branches.

While you relax, a gentle breeze stirs the leaves of the ancient oak tree, accompanied by the cooing of a dove. You also hear the trill of a warbler. Its song sounds like a flute with a series of high-pitched, rapid notes. Each note rises and falls in quick succession. These sounds are a reminder of the forest's vibrant ecosystem, a complex tapestry of life.

After a time, you rise and continue your walk, drawn towards a sunlit clearing ahead. As you enter the clearing, a breathtaking field of yellow and blue wildflowers in full bloom welcomes you. Yellow daisies, each with a chocolate-brown center, stand tall on slender stems that sway gently in the breeze, forming a sea of yellow. Amidst these flowers, cool pockets of blue make their presence known through delicate forget-me-nots. These tiny flowers, each only half an inch across, together with the daisies, create a stunning vision.

The air here is sweet with the scent of flowers. In the center of the clearing is a soft patch of grass, inviting you to lie down and gaze at the sky above.

Lie back and look up at the sky, now a brilliant shade of blue, completely clear of any clouds. The sun warms your skin, which relaxes your muscles. You scan your entire body as you lie on the ground, relaxing each part. Starting from your toes, moving to your legs, the middle of your body, your torso, your arms, your neck and then your head. You release any tension you've been holding.

As you lie here, your mind becomes as clear as the sky above. In this moment, there is only the here and now—the warmth of the sun, the softness of the grass, the gentle breeze. Embrace this feeling of peace.

Eventually, the sun begins its descent toward the horizon, signaling the end of the day. The sky transforms once more, this time into a scene of deepening blues streaked with the fiery oranges and reds of the setting sun. As you watch this magnificent display, you feel grateful for these beautiful sunsets with their vibrant colors.

Standing up from the grass, you make your way back through the forest. The path, illuminated by the golden light of sunset, appears different, yet remains strikingly beautiful. As nocturnal creatures begin their evening activities, the ambiance of the forest undergoes a shift. The chirping of crickets and the soft hoot of an owl blend with your footsteps, providing a calming backdrop to your return journey.

As you finish your walk, you notice a young deer among the trees. It stands still, its ears twitching at the slightest sound, alert to its surroundings. Once it seems satisfied with the safety of its space, it grazes, comfortable in the fading light. Observing its slender frame, the soft brown of its eyes, and the light brown coat, you find yourself captivated by its quiet grace.

Now it's time to leave this ancient forest. Come back to your current environment. Take the tranquility of the forest into your day or evening.

Journey 4: New England

Inhale slowly, counting to three, filling your lungs with air. Exhale gently, counting to three, releasing any tension. Repeat this process, taking three deep, purposeful breaths, allowing your body to relax more deeply with each one.

Imagine setting out for a summer weekend getaway in New England. The summer sun is bright and warm, perfect for a leisurely drive through the charming small towns of Massachusetts. You rent a convertible so you can experience the sunshine and salty ocean breeze while you drive.

The quaint and winding roads of New England usher you through picturesque towns steeped in history. These small towns feature charming shops, inviting restaurants, and centuries-old churches. As you pass by the town squares, you'll see large greens surrounded by several white churches with towering steeples along with older homes from the eighteenth century. These grassy areas once served as communal grazing spots for animals.

You stroll along one town green where two young children play a game of tag. They run quickly between the trees, smiling and laughing. A local person with a golden retriever strolls along the path. The dog, with its tail wagging, seems to smile at every passerby, while its owner exchanges a friendly nod with you.

You drive to a fishing village renowned for its delicious food. A small, local restaurant offers fresh fish and chips, lobster rolls, tasty sandwiches, and soups that you can smell as soon as you enter this cozy place. The meal is more than just food; it's a chance to experience the pleasure of summer. You relax and savor one of their specialties.

After lunch, you take a leisurely walk through the village, exploring its charming shops. Each storefront tells its own story. A fortune teller offers glimpses into the future. A small jewelry shop displays nautical-themed designs, a clothing store displays its one-of-a-kind pieces, and a confectionery tempts with their fudge and salt-water. You watch taffy being stretched and wound on a slowly spinning machine. The scents of fudge and taffy fill the surrounding air.

As you continue down the main street, you pass by a small shop where children are enjoying ice cream cones, the melting treat occasionally dripping onto the sidewalk. A little child in red shorts catches your eye with their bright smile as you pass by. Their happiness is contagious, a reminder of life's simple pleasures.

The road forks, leading you down a narrow path lined with wooden cottages. Their flower boxes hold pink, purple, and white flowers in abundant blooms. The scent of the flowers mingles with the salty air, creating a rich sensory experience.

At the road's end, you find yourself at a quaint pier, home to a fishing shack from the 1880s, reminiscent of an old red barn. Its walls are decorated with an array of colorful vintage buoys, varying in color and size. The shack, with its rustic charm, overlooks a harbor bustling with life—fishing boats, sailboats, and motorboats, each with its own story to tell.

Drawn to the wall of buoys, you find yourself captivated by a bright blue one. As you reach out and gently touch it, the buoy turns slightly, as if acknowledging your presence.

As the sun begins its gentle descent, the white fluffy clouds turn a light pink color. You head to an old New England inn near the water. The Inn stands proudly, its white facade and gabled roof a picture of classic Victorian elegance. The front porch, adorned with rocking chairs and hanging flower baskets, invites visitors to sit and unwind.

Stepping into the inn, you're greeted by the warm glow of the lobby, where antique furnishings and soft light transport you to another time. The wooden floors creak softly underfoot, each step a reminder of the many travelers who have passed through these halls. The subtle scent of freshly washed linens fills the air.

Your bedroom features an antique wooden bed crafted from rich dark wood. It's fitted with soft, plush bedding for a luxurious and restful sleep. A vintage nightstand holds a classic brass table lamp that casts a warm light. The floral-patterned wallpaper adds a touch of elegance. A comfortable armchair upholstered in a similar floral fabric sits by the window, offering a cozy nook.

After freshening up, you make your way to the inn's dining room for dinner. A small crystal chandelier and elegant wall sconces create an atmosphere of warmth. The aroma of freshly baked bread wafts through the air. After settling at your table, you indulge in classic New England fare. The innkeeper is warm as they ask about your day's activities while serving your meal.

After dinner, you explore the inn's grounds. The garden, illuminated by soft lanterns, offers pathways that lead you through beds of blooming flowers and manicured shrubs.

As the evening deepens, you return to the front porch of the inn, joining other guests who are enjoying the cool night air. Together, you watch the glittering stars appear in the clear night sky. The peaceful ambiance, coupled with the gentle rocking of the chairs and the soft conversations around you, lulls you into a state of deep relaxation.

Now it's time to come back to your present environment. Slowly open your eyes and bring this feeling of peacefulness into your day or evening.

Journey 5: Desert Beauty

Inhale slowly, counting to three, filling your lungs with air. Exhale gently, counting to three, releasing any tension. Repeat this process, taking three deep, purposeful breaths, allowing your body to relax more deeply with each one.

Imagine embarking on a journey to Arizona, known for its unique desert landscapes. As you arrive, you're struck by the vibrant life of this arid environment. The desert is teeming with huge cacti and other scrubby plants, each uniquely adapted to dry conditions.

You check into your hotel, eager to explore the surrounding area. As you walk along a pathway, you notice the earth beneath your feet is a deep red, creating a striking contrast against the clear blue sky. The scent of sage fills the air, providing an earthy aroma that heightens your connection to this place. As you wander, you come across towering cacti, some reaching up to twenty feet tall. These majestic plants are over one hundred years old, which fills you with awe. They are living testaments to the resilience of nature.

You venture through the scrubby landscape, past more of the giant cacti. Along the way, lizards, beetles, and birds dart away at your approach. Each creature plays a part in the desert's ecosystem. As you gaze downward, you notice the intricate patterns etched into the sand by the wind's gentle caress. The grains, like tiny jewels, shimmer in the sunlight. Embedded within this vast expanse are delicate footprints of creatures that have traversed this terrain long before your arrival. Some tracks are fresh, while others are ancient, weathered by time. As you walk, your feet press against the firm sand, and you feel the solidity of this arid terrain beneath you.

Your journey leads you to an area dotted with many holes about eight inches in diameter. Curious about the inhabitants of these burrows, you sit quietly. Before long, a prairie dog pops its head out of a hole. It's a charming creature, resembling a cross between a squirrel and a chipmunk, about a foot long, with a bushy tail like that of a small dog. As you watch in silence, more prairie dogs emerge, peeking out from their burrows. One larger prairie dog soon makes an appearance, darting from one hole to another. Watching these creatures, you feel a sense of joy and contentment, grateful that they do not feel threatened by you.

Retracing your steps, you head back to your hotel, a structure designed to blend in with the surrounding landscape. Its earthy hue is the same as the desert terrain, while its rounded edges mimic the natural contours of the land. The architecture evokes a sense of reverence for the indigenous peoples who once inhabited these lands, reminiscent of the traditional dwellings crafted from earth, sand, and stones.

That night, while you sleep, a gentle rain falls over the desert. You awaken to a transformed landscape—the cacti and scrubby plants appear rejuvenated. Some even sprout small red and yellow flowers. The desert's capacity for sudden transformation is impressive.

As you set out, the sounds of two distinct birds fill the air: the cactus wren and the Gila woodpecker. The cactus wren, cloaked in spotted and streaked brown feathers, blends into the surroundings, making it a challenge to spot. Its song, a lively series of chirps and trills, enlivens the atmosphere. In contrast, the Gila woodpecker, with its striking black and white back and a splash of red at the nape, is more visible. Its rhythmic drumming on cactus columns contributes a resonant backdrop to the morning soundscape.

You head towards large outcroppings resembling small mountains, their deep red soil characteristic of Arizona. As you explore, you stumble on a cave with a wide mouth. Stepping inside, you're pleasantly surprised by its coolness, a stark contrast to the desert heat. The cave, a natural wonder, offers a welcome respite and deepens your appreciation of the desert's hidden treasures.

Venturing further, you explore the narrow alleys that snake through these towering formations. These walls rise several stories high, leaving you in awe. You admire these gargantuan formations, marveling at their grandeur.

After walking through this natural labyrinth, you stop to rest and eat. The temperature is perfect, the air fresh and invigorating. As you look out over the horizon, you realize that the desert holds secrets only revealed to those who take the time to explore it. You breathe in deeply and feel gratitude for this beauty.

As the afternoon progresses and the sun sets, the sky transforms. Above, clouds gather, swelling with the promise of rain, their tops tinged with orange and pink hues, casting dramatic shadows on the desert floor.

As you continue your journey back to your hotel, the scent of creosote fills the air, mingling with the earthy aroma of impending rain. A gentle breeze whispers through the desert scrub, stirring the branches of mesquite trees and causing the sand to dance in swirls. Along the way, you see your prairie dog friends emerging from their burrows. Watching them scurry about, you're struck by their sweet and communal nature. You're sure they know it will rain soon.

A coolness fills the air, bringing a refreshing change from the heat of the day. The occasional rustle of a breeze through the brush or the distant call of an animal breaks the silence. As the first drops of rain fall, the desert seems to breathe a sigh of relief. The rain begins with a gentle touch as it brushes against your skin. Hurrying back to your hotel just before the downpour, you find refuge as the rain intensifies.

From your window, you watch the dance of raindrops on the desert landscape. Droplets form delicate patterns on the glass, tracing their journey downwards. The blurred view of the desert through the rain-spattered window creates a serene and beautiful sight.

Now it's time to leave the desert. When you're ready, take this feeling of peacefulness and wonder into your day or evening.

Journey 6: Hang Gliding

Inhale slowly, counting to three, filling your lungs with air. Exhale gently, counting to three, releasing any tension. Repeat this process, taking three deep, purposeful breaths, allowing your body to relax more deeply with each one.

Imagine you're an expert at hang gliding. Today's journey takes you to a breathtaking landscape—a picturesque valley with a meandering stream, nestled between small mountains. Below, expansive fields stretch out as far as the eye can see. The landscape is adorned with shades of emerald, sage, and olive, interspersed with patches of earthy browns where crops flourish. Surrounding these fields, the forest bursts with vibrant hues, as firs and conifers display an array of rich green colors, from deep, shadowy tones to bright shades. Interwoven among them, other trees add bursts of color, with their bright yellow, deep red, and fiery orange leaves. You appreciate this panoramic landscape, eager to glide into it.

You get ready for your flight at the edge of a small mountain. Clad in your helmet, with the large yellow hang glider snugly harnessed to your back, you inspect each part. Feeling the sturdy straps and buckles, you ensure everything is secure. The long sack trailing behind you will envelop your feet after takeoff. A gentle breeze touches your face—it's the perfect weather to fly. You gaze at the mountains in the distance with their rich, green forests and the expansive fields below.

Approaching the cliff's edge, you eagerly anticipate feeling the freedom of being in the air. With determination, you move towards the precipice and push off. The moment you leave the ground, a rush of exhilaration floods your senses. The cool air brushes against your skin. You swiftly tuck your feet into the sack, transitioning into a horizontal position. Soaring through the air, free from the constraints of the ground, you love the sensation of being a bird in human form.

You hear the rustle of the wing as it catches the breeze. Holding onto the textured glider bar, you navigate through the air. You feel weightless. The joy of flying gives you a sense of boundless freedom.

You enjoy the view of the world beneath you as you glide effortlessly over the valley. A patchwork of green fields stretches below, adorned with occasional yellow and purple wildflowers that add splashes of color to the fields. Each glance offers a unique view of the many textures and colors of the earth.

You gently guide your hang glider in a sweeping, circular path around the valley, enjoying the serenity of flight. The glider responds with grace to your touch, as if it, too, is in awe of the scenery. With each turn, a new aspect of the valley reveals itself. You appreciate the sight of rugged mountains ahead. The scruffy brush, the rich brown of the soil, and the stark gray of the rocks on this mountain face.

The air is fresh. You feel a lightness, both physically and mentally, as if you're part of the sky itself. As you glide, you see a gentle stream winding through the valley. Its waters meander through the landscape, carving a path that reflects the sunlight. You breathe in the clean air and appreciate the sight of the river wandering the valley beneath you.

As you glide along, a group of deer emerges from the forest's edge, making their way toward the stream. At the forefront strides a magnificent stag, his antlers branching out proudly. Following closely behind is a doe, her form elegant and slender, her coat a soft shade of tan. Her eyes, large and doe-like, exude a sense of gentleness and watchfulness as she guides her fawns towards the stream. Bringing up the rear is a playful fawn, its coat adorned with spots of white that shine. As the deer reach the water's edge, they drink, undisturbed by your presence above. They embody perfect calmness.

Beginning your descent towards a field, the view of the world below gradually sharpens. As you draw closer, the earthy scents of grass and soil drift upwards, welcoming you back to the ground. The blur of green transforms into distinct shapes, revealing individual bushes and plants.

As you prepare for landing, you ease your feet out of the sack. The moment your feet touch the earth, a satisfying thud resonates through you, anchoring you back to the ground. You carefully steady the glider and unhook yourself. A feeling of achievement and contentment washes over you.

In the distance, you see a small red fox. Its sleek, auburn fur glows in the sunlight, and its alert ears twitch. It glances at you and then trots off toward a clump of fir trees at the base of the mountain. You decide to stretch your legs, so you head toward the forested area where the fox went.

As you walk across the meadow, you're struck by the scent of fresh grass intermingled with a delicate hint of wildflowers. In the distance, a bird's melodic call echoes through the meadow, its song crisp and clear. The comforting murmur of the nearby stream adds to the chorus, its gentle babbling a constant reminder of the ever-flowing rhythm of life.

As you reach the edge of the forest, you look up at the sky. Fluffy white clouds drift lazily overhead. They seem to float effortlessly, casting fleeting shadows on the ground below. A large oblong cloud traverses the blue sky, while a circular cloud appears to follow in its wake. Smaller clouds trail behind. One has hints of gray in its billowing form while the next one is almost pure white. Together, they serve as a reminder of the infinite variety of the natural world.

Now it's time to leave the valley. Come back to your present environment and bring this feeling of tranquility into your day or evening.

Journey 7: Rose Garden

Inhale slowly, counting to three, filling your lungs with air. Exhale gently, counting to three, releasing any tension. Repeat this process, taking three deep, purposeful breaths, allowing your body to relax more deeply with each one.

Imagine you're standing on a stone walkway leading into a vast rose garden. Roses in raised beds border this pathway. Surrounding the garden are tall, lush green hedges, creating a secluded space, a world away from the hustle and bustle of daily life.

As you walk down this path, you notice the smooth beige stones underfoot—each one is a different size and shape, but they fit together well. The temperature is warm, and a light wind carries the subtle fragrance of the garden. With each step, a sense of serenity washes over you.

On your right is a row of large, light pink American roses. These flowers are heavy on their stems and seem to nod gently as you pass by. You walk over to one that's in full bloom. Each petal is slightly different, intricately woven into a compact design, a marvel of nature's artistry. This rose has a surprising number of petals—far more than initially apparent at first glance.

Bending closer, you inhale the strong, sweet scent of this rose. It fills your nostrils and lingers, a fragrance that speaks of summer days and the richness of life. It's no wonder that roses are so loved. The aroma is calming. You savor the scent and the beauty of this rose in front of you.

As you continue walking, you notice the diversity among the pink roses in this row. Some have multiple flowers, while others are at different stages of their life cycle. Some petals have fallen, carpeting the ground beneath in a soft pink blanket. A small rosebud reaches up toward the sun near some roses in full bloom.

Tall green wooden sticks support the rose bushes, ensuring they remain upright. The stems vary in shades of green, and you notice the thorns, perfect triangles, an essential part of the plant.

Next, you encounter yellow roses. You lean in, breathing deeply. Their scent is more subtle. The petals are satin-soft against your skin, a tactile reminder of their delicacy.

As you meander through the garden, the beauty of colors and fragrances captivates you. Each row introduces a different colored rose. The English white roses are next, their pure, creamy petals standing out like porcelain sculptures. Now you meet the vibrant red roses. Their deep crimson color is so rich it almost seems to pulse with life. Following the reds are the dark orange roses. These flowers are like bursts of sunset captured in petals, their fiery tones evoking warmth. Then come the light purple roses, elegant and mysterious. They evoke a sense of wonder with their soft lavender hue. As you walk in this garden, you are strolling through a living rainbow. Your pace slows. You feel the warmth of the sunshine on your face and breathe in the scent of these beautiful flowers.

Eventually, you encounter a green wooden bench, inviting you to rest. Small blue birds flit from one side of the garden to the other, providing vibrant bursts of color. These birds, known as Blue Tits, boast striking blue and yellow feathers. Their white faces and distinct dark eye lines captivate you as they dart about while cheerfully chirping.

After a while, you rise from the bench and head towards the other side of the garden. A new pathway appears, adorned with a trellis covered in red roses. This path veers off, guiding you towards an unexpected sight: a sculpture garden nestled inside walls of meticulously manicured shrubs.

As you enter the sculpture garden, the first piece to capture your attention is a striking sculpture of a queen. Cast in bronze, she stands regally on a stone pedestal. Her gaze is serene yet commanding. Adorned in elegant attire, she wears an ornate dress and flowing robes, with a majestic crown. Purple and white flower beds surround her, a floral homage that enhances her majesty.

Next to the queen, a playful scene unfolds in a bronze sculpture depicting a dog and a cat. The dog, with its tail mid-wag, seems to invite the cat into a game, while the cat stands back, poised with a mix of curiosity and caution. You touch the dog's brass tail and the cat's face. You can imagine these were beloved companions of the queen.

Further along the path, you come upon the sculpture of a king in bronze. He stands tall and proud, his posture relaxed yet authoritative. Clad in regal attire, with a scepter in one hand and the other resting on a sword, he embodies the qualities of leadership and strength. The king's face, detailed with a wise and gentle expression, suggests he may have been a benevolent ruler. Positioned opposite the queen, you can imagine these sculptures talking to one another.

In one corner, you find a sculpture depicting a young princess. Crafted from marble, she stands gracefully on a stone pedestal, exuding an air of elegance and poise. Adorned in a flowing gown, you imagine she might be just ten or eleven years old. A delicate tiara graces her head. Surrounding the princess sculpture, a cluster of blooming pink rose bushes adds a touch of color to the scene.

In another part of the garden, a surprise awaits: a whimsical sculpture of a fairy sitting atop a mushroom. The artist created her wings with translucent material that catches the light. This unexpected element adds a touch of fantasy, and you marvel at her joyful expression.

Now it's time to leave the garden. Come back to your present environment and take this feeling of serenity into your day or evening.

Journey 8: Forest Waterfall

Inhale slowly, counting to three, filling your lungs with air. Exhale gently, counting to three, releasing any tension. Repeat this process, taking three deep, purposeful breaths, allowing your body to relax more deeply with each one.

Imagine you're in an ancient forest, walking along a meandering pathway. Towering fir trees stand tall, their majestic, conical silhouettes and dark-green needles reaching into the skyline. Robust oak trees, with their broad, gnarled limbs, stretch outward with their deep green leaves. Delicate birches add contrast with their distinctive white bark and fluttering bright green leaves. Mighty pines stand alongside, displaying their long, slender needles. The sun glints through the many leaves, creating patterns of light and shadow. You admire this beautiful scene.

You wander along, feeling the soft, packed trail. Occasionally, you hear the crunch of a stick or dried leaf underfoot. Ferns and other flora border the path, which winds between ancient trees. You take a deep breath, filling your lungs with the crisp, clean air, scented lightly with the earthy aroma of the surrounding plants and trees.

Continuing down the path, the faint sound of water greets your ears. The trail slopes downward, leading you to a clearing where a vast waterfall plunges into a wide pool below. As you draw nearer, the forceful sound of water crashing against the rocks and flowing into the basin becomes more prominent.

The rocks vary in size and shape, creating a multitude of mini waterfalls inside the larger cascade. Leaves, twigs, and occasionally small branches get caught in the flow, embarking on a swift journey over the edge. A leaf spirals in the air for a moment, catching a droplet of mist, before getting swept into the pool below. Twigs navigate the currents with a bobbing motion, sometimes getting momentarily lodged between rocks, vibrating under the force of the water, before being dislodged and continuing their trip.

Rocks rest along the edges of the waterfall—worn smooth in places by the relentless flow. They glisten with moisture, their surfaces occasionally obscured by the rushing water. Bubbles and foam gather at the base of the waterfall, creating a momentary appearance of soap suds.

Around the waterfall, the air becomes heavier and more humid from the mist of the cascade. Surrounding this natural marvel, clusters of small trees and lush bushes thrive, their foliage adorned with droplets, shimmering as though dusted with jewels. As you reach out to touch a plant near the path's edge, the cool dampness against your skin is refreshing. You inhale deeply, experiencing air rich with humidity and the scent of moist earth.

The waterfall pours into a clear, deep green pool. Here, the water seems to rest momentarily, gathering itself before flowing onward. You dip your hands in this pool, moving them back and forth, feeling the weight and flow of the cool water around your fingers.

As you resume your walk, you follow the water as it winds through the forest and becomes a small stream. As the sun filters through the trees, the waters sparkle under the sun's rays. You appreciate how clear and pure the water appears and to hear its gurgles as it makes its way through the forest.

In some sections, the stream narrows because of rocks and fallen trees, forcing the water to quicken its pace and produce a babbling brook. In contrast, wider parts of the stream slow down, allowing the water to flow with a gentle, lazy rhythm. Here, the surface of the water reflects the surrounding foliage and sky. The bed of the stream is a mosaic of pebbles and stones, contributing to the varied sounds of the water's flow.

You lean over to pick up some stones from the shallow water. The stones are cool to the touch, their surfaces smoothed by years of being worn down. Among them, you find small rocks in a variety of colors—ranging from deep, slate gray to warm, russet browns and even some with veins of white or flecks of mica.

As you examine the stones, you notice the subtle differences in texture and weight. One brown stone is perfectly round, polished by the relentless tumbling, while a gray stone with flecks of white is almost triangular. Another similar rock with the same coloring is jagged, and you wonder if these two rocks were once part of a larger piece. The biggest stone is the color of rust, and it is flat and oblong. These different shapes reveal the interaction between water and stone. They are a testament to the slow but powerful forces of nature, shaping and refining each stone over time.

You gaze at the aquatic plants anchored among the stones. Their roots grasp the pebbles, securing a foothold in the dynamic environment of the stream. Their slender stems reach upwards from the streambed, adorned with vibrant green leaves that vary in shape and size. Some leaves are broad and oval, while others are slender and needle-like.

As the plants sway gently in the current, their leaves undulate gracefully, adding to the dynamic beauty of the underwater landscape. Their lush foliage provides hiding places for small fish and other aquatic creatures. Over time, these plants play a crucial role in stabilizing the stream bank and maintaining water quality, contributing to the overall health of this environment.

You gently place the brown, gray, and rust-colored stones back into the water, so they continue to contribute to the stream's ecosystem. You listen to the sound of each one falling to the bottom.

Now it's time to leave this beautiful forest. Come back to your current environment. Take a few deep breaths in and then let them out slowly. Bring this peaceful feeling into your day or evening.

Journey 9: Cornwall Coast

Inhale slowly, counting to three, filling your lungs with air. Exhale gently, slowly counting to three, releasing any tension. Repeat this process, taking three deep, purposeful breaths, allowing your body to relax more deeply with each exhale.

Imagine embarking on a journey along the picturesque English coast in Cornwall, a place known for its breathtaking views of the ocean with paths that wind along the countryside through many towns and idyllic pastures.

Your journey begins with a train ride to a quaint inn, a four-hundred-year-old building with a rustic thatched roof, nestled in the heart of the countryside. The narrow roads in that area have signs that point proudly to different towns nearby. As you make your way to the inn, you catch sight of several quaint cottages, built of red brick or gray stone, which have stood for hundreds of years. You take in a deep breath of the fresh country air and head into the inn.

Your room is cozy, with exposed wooden beams and furnishings that look antique but are surprisingly comfortable. You touch the smooth wood and soft light-colored fabrics of this furniture. Exhausted from your journey, you easily drift into a deep sleep in a bed that feels tailor-made for you.

As dawn breaks, you awaken to the delightful aroma of home-cooked food wafting through the air—freshly baked breads, perfectly cooked eggs, an array of fruits, and an assortment of pastries. Sitting down to a hearty breakfast, you enjoy each bite, nourishing your body for the day's hike. The dining room is small with wooden furniture that shows its wear, but the atmosphere is convivial, and you relax as you savor your breakfast.

With a sense of anticipation, you begin your hike along the winding coastal path, which is found near your inn. The trail meanders along the hilly shore, dotted with scrubby green brush, each step offering a new perspective of the stunning Cornish landscape and the ocean off in the distance. Soon, you enter a forest. The path, narrow yet well-trodden, leads you beneath a covering of trees, their leaves filtering the sunlight and casting abstract pictures of light on the ground. The gentle rustle of leaves accompanies you, brushing gently against you as you walk. You gaze at the sunlight on the forest floor and listen to the surrounding sounds.

Emerging from the forest, you come upon a field. Climbing over a post, you enter a farmer's pasture. Families of sheep graze peacefully, the curious lambs turning their heads in your direction, yet staying close to their parents. You hear a few muted 'baahs' and smell the scent of grass around you. The small lambs watch you as you traverse the field.

You continue onward, crossing another pasture, where cows, unfazed by your presence, continue to graze. A few are sitting down in the field. They seem contented to be there and you feel the same way. You notice their slow, deliberate movements and large dark eyes.

As you walk, the path leaves the fields and becomes slightly more rugged. Small stones and natural debris crunch underfoot. Feel the texture of the ground changing. The trail ascends slightly, and you find your heart rate increasing with the effort. You breathe deeply and smell a slight saltiness in the air.

The trail eventually brings you to the edge of a majestic cliff, where the vast ocean stretches out before you, its surface a shimmering expanse that merges with the horizon. The sky is a brilliant blue, dotted with a few swiftly moving clouds. Below, the ocean is calm, with seabirds gliding gracefully from the cliff toward the water. Gulls dive for fish while others float lazily on the gentle waves. To your left, a small white ship sails slowly, a solitary traveler on the ocean. The chalky white cliffs plummet beneath you in a steep descent, presenting a rugged landscape. You sit down to marvel at all the surrounding beauty and breathe in the ocean air.

Your hike continues until you reach a quaint village. There, you stop at a small pub for lunch and a drink, a welcome respite after your morning walk. The meal is simple yet delicious; the fresh air and your recent exercise enhances the flavors. You strike up a conversation with a few local folks, who kindly direct you to the next village, assuring you of continued pleasant weather. Their friendly demeanor and helpful advice bring a smile to your face.

Rejuvenated, you resume your hike. The path cuts through scrubby underbrush and weaves past a couple of large stone buildings that look as if they're ancient farms that are still in operation. You pass through several empty fields and walk by a few small brick cottages.

The path then veers to the right, leading you back toward the ocean. The rhythmic movement of the waves, combined with the bright blue sky set over a sapphire ocean, creates a scene of unparalleled beauty. In the distance, you see a few people walking, and the welcoming appearance of a nearby village with its old stone buildings that cluster around a small harbor.

As you stand there, lost in the beauty of Cornwall, a small white rabbit emerges from its hole. The breeze ruffles its silky fur as it busily hops and runs about. You sit down, not wanting to disturb the rabbit's playful exploration. Then, noticing your presence, the rabbit approaches and sits nearby. Together, you both enjoy the gentle breeze, the breathtaking sunset, and the comfortable temperature, sharing a moment of quiet companionship.

In this serene moment, time seems to slow down. The rabbit also gazes out at the horizon, its small body relaxed and at ease. The scene is almost magical, as if lifted from the pages of a storybook. You feel a deep connection to this simple creature who isn't afraid of you. It eventually eats some of the grass and then hops away.

The peacefulness of the countryside, the rhythmic sound of the waves, and the many colors of the landscape have all combined to create a beautiful vista. For centuries, countless individuals have walked this path, and you feel fortunate to be experiencing it today.

It's time to go back to the inn, so you return on the same route. You pass the sheep's pasture, which is now empty, head through the forest, and then back toward the inn. The path back is familiar now, and you recognize large stones, certain plants, and trees that you saw earlier. The air is cool, a gentle reminder of the day's transition into late afternoon.

Arriving back, you feel a sense of deep contentment wash over you. The inn, with its warm lights glowing softly against the evening sky and the comforting scent of a crackling fire drifting through the air, beckons you. Stepping inside, you're enveloped by the cozy embrace of its centuries-old walls. As you make your way to the dining area, your stomach rumbles in anticipation of the evening meal. You settle into a worn wooden chair at a table with flickering candles, eager to indulge in the culinary delights of the region.

Soon, plates piled high with locally sourced ingredients are placed before you. Succulent roast beef and chicken, accompanied by buttery new potatoes and tender garden vegetables harvested from the inn's own garden. Each bite presents delicious flavors that celebrate the rich culinary heritage of Cornwall.

Now it's time to leave the inn. Come back to your current environment. Take a moment to feel your fingers and toes. When you're ready, take this feeling of contentment into your day or evening.

Journey 10: Taj Mahal

Inhale slowly, counting to three, filling your lungs with air. Exhale gently, counting to three, releasing any tension. Repeat this process, taking three deep, purposeful breaths, allowing your body to relax more deeply with each one.

Imagine you are in India, embarking on a journey to visit the Taj Mahal, one of the seven wonders of the world. Your journey takes you on country roads through small villages and expansive fields, offering glimpses of daily life in India. Traffic is chaotic, but you feel safe with your driver. You stop for chai and enjoy the milky tea, which is one of the treats of this country.

As you approach Agra, your anticipation builds. You arrive at the entrance, where a magnificent red sandstone building, the royal gate, stands in front of the Taj Mahal. This square building, crowned with an enormous dome, boasts intricate inlays of white marble and precious stones that create delicate floral designs on the exterior. The four red sandstone towers at each corner, crowned with elegant cupolas, add to the majesty of the gateway. This impressive structure momentarily obscures the Taj Mahal, but as you draw closer, glimpses of the amazing monument reveal themselves through the large entryway.

As you pass through the Royal Gate, a breathtaking view of the Taj Mahal greets you. You can see the building's perfect reflection in the long, narrow pool that leads to it. The sky is a clear, brilliant blue, creating a stunning backdrop for the white marble of the Taj Mahal, which appears to float above its reflection.

You walk alongside the reflecting pool, taking in the grandeur of this place. The Taj Mahal sits majestically on an elegant marble platform with four large cylindrical towers on each corner, framing the elegant structure. The building has a massive central dome with four smaller domes surrounding it. Below the enormous dome is a grand archway, and beneath the smaller domes are additional archways, creating a beautiful symmetry. You gaze at this beautiful and wondrous building from far away and appreciate its reflection in the long pool.

Reaching the base of the Taj Mahal, the sheer scale of the structure strikes you. Standing 240 feet tall (73 meters), it reaches up into the air. You listen to a nearby tour guide recounting the history of this magnificent mausoleum built in the 1600s by

Emperor Shah Jahan in memory of his beloved wife Mumtaz Mahal, who died during childbirth. Both Shah Jahan and Mumtaz Mahal are laid to rest here. This building is a testament to their great love.

As you draw closer to the entrance, the intricate details of the Taj Mahal become apparent. The white marble walls are inlaid with elaborate blue and red floral designs. Skilled workers created these intricate patterns of dancing flowers, creeping vines, and delicate plants using different-colored gems. They're a testament to the extraordinary craftsmanship of the Mughal artisans. From a distance, these designs appear as symmetrical patterns, but up close, you see their detail. It's clear that many artisans spent a great deal of time creating every element of this building.

You enter the main building, where the burial chambers of Shah Jahan and Mumtaz Mahal reside. The interior is a stark contrast. A small, dark, and quiet room with their tombs exudes a sense of peace and reverence. Standing in this intimate space, you reflect on the beauty of the building and the love story it symbolizes.

Leaving the interior, you walk around the massive structure, taking in the views of the Yamuna River flowing lazily nearby. The brown river contrasts with the pristine marble of the Taj Mahal. You visit each corner of the base, looking up at the towering columns, each one 137 feet high (43 meters). Their imposing height and intricate design are a testament to the architectural genius of the Mughal era.

Returning to the reflecting pool, you find a bench and take a seat, allowing yourself a moment to absorb the majesty of the Taj Mahal. The sky, now dotted with gray clouds, reflects beautifully in the shimmering water.

As you sit there, the sounds of Agra envelop you. The conversation of other visitors, children yelling and laughing, the gentle rustle of the wind through the gardens all display how this is a place that is very alive. The contrast between the vibrant life outside and the peaceful solemnity within the building's walls is striking.

You stand and walk towards the gardens that surround the Taj Mahal. The architects laid out these gardens in a symmetrical pattern, dividing them into four equal parts. Each quadrant of the garden is a mirror image of the other. As you explore them, you encounter the tall, slender cypress trees and a variety of fruit trees. Fragrant flowers like roses and jasmine thrive in this garden, making it a peaceful retreat. This carefully curated blend of plants adds to the beauty of the setting.

The gardens are alive with the colors of India—the bright greens of the manicured lawns, the vibrant hues of the flowers, and the soft blue of the sky reflecting on the long pools. The symmetry of the gardens, with their geometric precision, contrasts beautifully with the natural, free-flowing grace of the plants and trees.

You sit on another bench, near a reflecting pool within the gardens. The water's surface is still, acting as a mirror. You watch as a gentle breeze creates ripples across the water, distorting and then restoring the reflected image of the Taj Mahal. It's a moment of contemplation, a time to reflect on the beauty and impermanence of life.

Leaving the gardens, you circle back towards the main entrance, taking one last look at the Taj Mahal.

Now it's time to leave this wonder of the world. Come back to your current environment and take a deep breath. Feel your fingers and toes. Take this feeling of wonder and contentment into your day or evening.

Journey 11: Beach Resort

Inhale slowly, counting to three, filling your lungs with air. Exhale gently, counting to three, releasing any tension. Repeat this process, taking three deep, purposeful breaths, allowing your body to relax more deeply with each one.

Imagine you've just arrived at a luxurious beach resort, a picturesque oasis, nestled on a pristine coastline, with the sea stretching out before you. The moment you step onto the soft, white sand, a sense of calm washes over you. The air carries the fresh, salty scent of the sea, and a gentle breeze caresses your skin.

You make your way to your room, a haven of tranquility and luxury. The most stunning feature awaits you here: a glass-bottom floor that offers a view of the ocean's depths. As you step onto the transparent floor, a vibrant underwater world reveals itself. Schools of colorful fish swim gracefully beneath your feet, their scales shimmering in the sunlight filtering through the water. The hues are breathtaking—brilliant blues, radiant yellows, vivid oranges, and deep purples. You pause to appreciate these beautiful creatures.

The water's gentle movements create many views of the ocean. You see underwater plants swaying softly, with fish darting in and around them. A small sea turtle moves at a sluggish pace before disappearing.

After relaxing in your room, you put on some swimwear, ready to embrace the beach experience. You find the perfect spot to relax—a white cloth chair under a colorful striped blue and white umbrella, which offers a view of the shimmering sea. It's a quiet spot where you can appreciate your surroundings.

You settle into the chair, allowing yourself to fully relax in the day's warmth. Occasionally, a breeze sweeps in that cools your skin. You appreciate the balance of warmth with the refreshing touch of the breeze.

A fluffy white cloud drifts lazily across the clear blue sky, transforming shapes as it travels. The rhythmic sound of waves rolling onto the shore fills the air. Each wave is followed by a gentle retreat. You listen intently to the water visiting the sand, a soft swoosh followed by a subtle hiss as each wave pulls back, never quite repeating the same pattern. These sounds tell a story of the sea's perpetual motion.

After some time, you take a walk along the beach. The sand near the water is cool under your bare feet. A pleasant contrast to the warmth of the sun. As you stroll along the shoreline, the gentle waves occasionally wash over your feet, a refreshing sensation.

As you wander down the beach, you pass two children giggling as they build an elaborate sandcastle. A few people are swimming in the surf while groups stand at the edge of the water, their conversation mingling with the sounds of the sea. Further down, a group of friends plays a lively game of Frisbee. One person hurls an orange frisbee at their friend, who grins when they catch it.

After a leisurely walk, you return to your chair, settling back under the shade of the umbrella. From this vantage point, you watch a seagull as it lands nearby, strutting along the beach with an air of curiosity before taking flight once again. You relish the feeling of having nothing to do but relax and soak in the beauty of your surroundings.

As you gaze out at the ocean, you become entranced by the waves. Each one is unique, yet they all follow a rhythmic pattern. Smaller waves gently roll in, followed by larger ones that crash onto the shore with more force and energy. The combination of the waves' soothing sounds and the distant calls of seagulls is calming.

In this tranquil state, you pick up a book you've been wanting to read. Time stands still as you become absorbed in the story, the words transporting you to another world. You forget where you are for a while.

As the afternoon lazily drifts along, a hotel attendant approaches, offering you a refreshing drink and a light snack. You gratefully accept. Soon you're sipping a cold beverage and enjoying a delicious treat. You continue reading your book, wondering what will happen next in the story.

As the sun begins its descent towards the horizon, the sky transforms from bright blue to shades of orange and amber. Wisps of clouds, tinged now with pink and gold, drift lazily across the sky. The ocean and sand, bathed in the soft, golden light, take on a radiant glow. And as the air cools, the hotel attendant kindly provides you with a light blanket to keep warm, ensuring you can continue to enjoy the sunset.

As it sinks below the horizon, the sun seems to dissolve into the ocean, leaving behind a glistening trail of light on the water. The orange sky reflects off the waves, turning the ocean into a pool of liquid gold. As the sun disappears, the sky darkens, transitioning to deep purple and dark blue.

Nightfall brings a new ambiance to the beach. The once vibrant landscape is now bathed in the soft, serene light of dusk. The ocean, now a deep inky blue, whispers secrets of the night as the waves continue their eternal dance. You stand up, feeling a deep sense of peace and rejuvenation, ready to return to your room.

Now it's time to leave this exclusive resort. Come back to your present environment. Feel your fingers and toes along with the rest of your body. Take this feeling of calm with you into your day or evening.

Journey 12: Egyptian Pyramids

Inhale slowly, counting to three, filling your air with lungs. Exhale gently, counting to three, releasing any tension. Repeat this process, taking three deep, purposeful breaths, allowing your body to relax more deeply with each one.

Imagine you are on a trip to Egypt, a land of ancient wonders. Your journey begins with a flight to Cairo, the vibrant heart of the country, where the past and present merge. As you descend into the city, the sprawling urban landscape gives way to the awe-inspiring sight of the Great Pyramids, rising majestically on the horizon, about twelve miles (twenty kilometers) from the bustling city center.

On your first morning in Cairo, an expert guide greets you clad entirely in white. The pyramids reside on the city's outskirts and your guide chauffeurs you to the Giza Plateau, where the iconic structures stand. Stepping out of the vehicle, these ancient wonders amaze you.

You're impressed by the monumental size of the Pyramid of Giza. Its triangular structure towers at 481 feet (146 meters). This pyramid, along with the equally impressive Pyramids of Khafre and Menkaure, has stood for over four thousand years.

Your guide explains these structures were created with over five million limestone blocks, quarried and transported from far away. The stones, weighing an average of two and one-half tons, were brought here without the use of wheeled vehicles. The Great Pyramid's original exterior stones, remnants of the polished limestone that once made the pyramid shine brilliantly under the sun, served as a symbol of the Pharoah's power.

As your gaze drifts to the Pyramid of Khafre, slightly smaller but standing on higher ground, it appears taller, which is an optical illusion. You step back and see these three ancient pyramids, surrounded by the endless expanse of sand, the many people, and large camels with their long slender legs. Picture the countless blocks, each telling a story of ancient workers who toiled long hours.

The air around the pyramids is hot and dry, filled with the scents of spices and roasted coffee from nearby vendors. Camel handlers, offering rides on their animals adorned with colorful blankets, add to the vibrant atmosphere. The camels emit loud, throaty noises. You take in this scene and feel the warmth of the sun on your face.

Your guide takes you inside the Great Pyramid of Giza, where you navigate through the long, narrow passageway known as the Grand Gallery. This corridor stretches approximately 157 feet (48 meters) in length and rises to a height of about twenty-eight feet (8.6 meters). The Gallery is characterized by its walls, where successive layers of stone are laid closer together as they rise, creating a stepped, inverted V-shape that narrows towards the ceiling.

You follow this narrow passageway up to the King's Chamber. It is an enormous room constructed of pink granite. Standing in this ancient room, you're amazed that you've traveled to a building erected over 4,000 years ago.

Exiting the pyramid, you head toward another of Egypt's iconic monuments: the Sphinx. This enigmatic statue, with its human head and lion's body, sits at a short distance from the pyramid. The sight of this ancient guardian is indeed overwhelming, with its enormous paws poised in majesty and the remnants of a splendid headdress hinting at its past grandeur. Your guide explains the Sphinx was built to protect the sacred tombs and temple complexes, which adds to the aura of mystery surrounding it. You admire this unusual tan-colored statue.

The next day marks the beginning of a new adventure—a Nile River cruise. As you board a small but luxurious boat, you're greeted by an expert crew and staff. As the boat glides along the Nile, you're treated to a panorama of life along the riverbanks. From your seat on the deck, with a cold drink in hand, you see people fishing in small boats, children playing along the water's edge, and traditional mud-brick homes. These buildings with their flat roofs and distinctive sandy hue, blending seamlessly into the environment. Here and there, the minarets of mosques reach towards the sky, their calls to prayer echoing softly across the water.

Your first stop is the Temple of Dendera, dedicated to the goddess Hathor. This rectangular building has towering columns throughout. You walk through an entrance with walls covered in hieroglyphs. The walls of this temple feature rich carvings, including notable depictions of Cleopatra VII and her son by Julius Caesar, Ptolemy XV, also known as Caesarion.

The hieroglyphics etched into the passageways captivate you. You see a falcon, symbolizing Horus, a major Egyptian deity. Horus embodies the divine qualities of strength, power, and vigilance. This deity is the protector of the pharaoh and the defender of the ancient Egyptian concept of truth, justice, and cosmic order. Horus symbolizes the eternal struggle between good and evil, light and darkness.

The walls also display scenes of elaborate ceremonial practices. Processions of priests and priestesses wearing robes carry offerings of food, flowers, and incense to appease the gods and ensure the prosperity of the land. You admire the scenes of music and dance, vividly capturing musicians with lyres and harps along with dancers who seem to come to life on the wall.

The next destination on your cruise is the Luxor Temple, a site of monumental significance. You arrive at sunset, the golden light casting a magical glow over the temple's large columns and vast courtyards. One courtyard impresses you with its tall figurines, who stand with crossed arms and serene expressions.

The figures wear traditional royal attire—the striped headdress that frames the face and gracefully falls over the shoulders. They also wear the iconic false beard, symbolizing Pharaonic divinity. The intricate details of their jewelry, such as collars and bracelets, are also visible. You marvel at the artisans' ability to work stone as if it were as malleable as gold.

After your wondrous day, you return to your boat on the Nile. The gentle rocking of the vessel and the soothing sound of the water create a perfect atmosphere for reflection. As you sit on the deck, gazing at the star-filled sky and the river, you feel a deep sense of connection to the ancient world.

The following days of your Nile cruise are filled with more wonders. You explore the Valley of the Kings, where pharaohs were laid to rest in ornate tombs carved into the desert hills. The walls of these sacred spaces display paintings that depict detailed portrayals of farming, hunting, feasting, and making music, showcasing the Egyptians' love for life and their belief in its continuation beyond death.

Stepping into the Temple of Karnak, you see the colossal Great Hypostyle Hall, where many towering columns rise dramatically. Each one contains hieroglyphs narrating tales of gods and pharaohs. Ram-headed sphinxes line the processional way. They silently guard the sacred paths once walked by priests and royalty.

As your time in Egypt comes to an end, you spend your last evening sitting by the Nile, marveling at the boats smoothly sailing past. You consider the countless individuals who have traversed this river for centuries. The river, a lifeline of this ancient land, flows quietly, carrying its history and legend.

Now it's time to leave Egypt. Come back to your present environment and bring this sense of peacefulness and wonder into your day or evening.

Journey 13: Winter Walk

Inhale slowly, counting to three, filling your lungs with air. Exhale gently, counting to three, releasing any tension. Repeat this process, taking three deep, purposeful breaths, allowing your body to relax more deeply with each one.

Picture a crisp, winter day. You decide to enjoy the outdoors with a leisurely stroll. A soft layer of snow blankets the ground, inviting you to embark on a journey down an old, quaint country road that leads into a dense evergreen forest.

You put on your cozy jacket, sturdy boots, and warm hat and gloves. As you step outside, the brisk chill brushes against your cheeks—a refreshing feeling, yet you feel comfortably shielded from the cold.

You make your way to a country road, noticing the fresh tracks from snowmobile enthusiasts who've crafted a narrow path for you. The sunlight touches your face as you step onto the snowy trail. A rustic fence on either side of this small road divides a pasture on your left from a group of trees on your right. You pause for a moment to absorb the tranquil scene around you.

The snow crunches beneath your boots as you walk. Strolling down this charming road, you notice the snow's gentle accumulation along the tops of the wooden fence timbers. Glancing down, you spot various animal tracks skirting the fence line—perhaps left by a curious rabbit or another small woodland creature.

You're struck by the unique way snow decorates the landscape. Over the fence on the pasture, a smattering of wild grass defiantly pierces through the snow. It gathers in soft mounds, sculpted by the whims of the wind. The sunlight glitters off the snow, creating dazzling bright spots.

As you proceed, the variety of trees catches your eye. Barren maple trees, their branches heavy with snow, starkly contrast with the lively evergreens, flaunting a spectrum of vibrant greens. The snow delicately clings to the evergreens, forming intricate patterns. Their vivid green hue stands out sharply against the white snow and the brilliant blue sky.

The country road soon gives way to a forest thick with fir and pine trees, where sunbeams play hide and seek through the tree canopy, casting a mosaic of light and shadow on the forest floor.

This dappled sunlight invites you to pause once more, breathing in the air's purity, and reveling in the moment's beauty.

Venturing deeper into the forest, the path narrows, and the lively chatter of birds fills the air. They flit about, busily foraging, their songs coming from different parts of the forest. You can occasionally see the bright red feathers of a cardinal, the flutter of sparrows, and other birds for a moment. You marvel at their resilience, thriving in this winter landscape.

The path meanders out of the woods and onto another open field bordered by a fence. It skirts a quaint farm, passing by a bright red barn adorned with icicles hanging along its roofline. The icicles, in their varied sizes, glisten as they catch the sunlight, their melting droplets creating small circular indentations in the snow-covered ground. You stand here for a moment, watching the drip of the largest icicle along the corner of the building.

As you continue past the barn, you follow a road that leads to a picturesque town filled with Victorian homes. Among them, an elegant pink house stands out, its rectangular shape adorned with intricate woodwork, ornate gables, and delicate white gingerbread trim along the porch. Despite its modest size, perhaps a cozy two-bedroom home, it exudes charm and character. Lace curtains adorn the windows, and a warm, inviting light spills from within, promising a haven of warmth and comfort to anyone who steps through its door.

Next to it, a house painted in a cheerful yellow, starkly contrasted with navy trim, stands out. The front door, crafted from carved wood and featuring a large stained-glass window, catches the light and scatters colorful patterns onto the snow.

A faint smell of wood smoke fills the air, a comforting and familiar scent. The smoke wisps gracefully from the chimneys, blending with the crisp winter air and adding to this idyllic setting. You breathe in the scents and appreciate the beauty of this environment.

You continue along this main road that leads to a cluster of shops, including a cozy coffee shop where the warmth inside has fogged up the windows. Enticed by the inviting scents of coffee, hot chocolate, and tea, you step inside.

The warmth envelops you immediately, a stark contrast to the chill you've left behind. The interior reminds you of a Swiss chalet with its polished wooden walls and rustic tables. It's a welcoming retreat. The air is rich with the aroma of various hot beverages—cider, chocolate, and coffee—mingling together, creating a comforting atmosphere. Laughter and chatter fill the space. A group of children bundled in their winter gear enjoy hot chocolate, while adults nearby savor their coffee and tea.

You order your favorite drink and find a seat near the window, where the condensation forms rivulets down the glass. Outside, the world passes by in a blur of colors and shapes, a beautiful backdrop to this moment of warmth and relaxation. Cradling your drink, you take a sip, allowing the warmth of the mug, the flavors, and the ambiance to fill you with a sense of contentment.

Now it's time to leave this winter wonderland. Come back to your present environment, carrying this feeling of peacefulness and warmth into the rest of your day or evening.

Journey 14: Hot Air Balloon

Inhale slowly, counting to three, filling your lungs with air. Exhale gently, counting to three, releasing any tension. Repeat this process, taking three deep, purposeful breaths, allowing your body to relax more deeply with each one.

Imagine you are going to take a ride in a hot-air balloon. Your journey begins as you're driven to a remote rural area in the early morning. It's still dark outside.

As you arrive, the sight of two magnificent hot-air balloons captures your attention. They are colossal, each standing about seventy feet high (twenty-one meters) and fifty-five feet wide (seventeen meters), rivaling the height of a seven-story building.

The darkness accentuates the silhouettes of the balloons against the starry backdrop. Each balloon seems to emit a soft glow from within, casting an ethereal light that illuminates its surroundings. You realize it's the flame nestled within each balloon, igniting and filling the chamber with hot air, that creates this beautiful sight.

Their vibrant colors and intricate geometric designs are striking against the night sky. Ropes tether each corner of the balloons to the ground, anchoring them before their ascent. The night air is crisp, carrying with it the earthy scents of the countryside.

A sense of anticipation builds as a few other passengers arrive, each sharing your sense of excitement and wonder. You climb into the spacious basket of one balloon. Divided into two compartments, the basket can hold eight people in each section. The atmosphere is one of adventure, with passengers exchanging smiles with you.

The balloon operator, a seasoned expert, instructs the ground crew to unhook the balloon from its ties. As the operator ignites the propane flame beneath the balloon's opening, a gentle warmth fills the air. You feel the basket rise, ascending slowly into the dark, pre-dawn sky. The second balloon also begins its ascent, floating gracefully in front of you.

Gradually, you rise above the treetops, carried by the wind. The sensation is one of utter weightlessness, as if you and the balloon are a part of the air itself. Ascending to a height of about 1,500 feet (457 meters), you float over a patchwork of fields, small houses, and winding country roads. You feel the chill air around you, but it's invigorating, and you take a deep breath of this clean air.

As the sun rises, the horizon transforms. The dark sky gradually gives way to the first hints of dawn's light. The golden sun peeks out, casting a warm, soft glow over the landscape. Over the next half hour, the sky becomes suffused with light, painting the other balloon with golden shades. You admire this extraordinary view.

Floating in the balloon, you experience a profound sense of peace. The quiet is occasionally broken by the sound of the propane flame, a brief roar that sends more heat into the balloon, gently lifting it higher. Mostly, however, the journey is filled with a blissful silence, providing a rare opportunity to feel you are part of the sky.

Floating above the landscape, you see fields where cows, horses, and goats graze freely. A farmhouse is off in the distance. From your elevated perspective, the world transforms into a miniature scene. Trees, bushes, and buildings shrink to toy-like proportions, while the animals meander like tiny figurines. Below, you notice a small family tending to their field beside a stone house, with their dog playing nearby.

As you drift closer to a quaint cluster of homes nestled in the rural landscape, you see several children below. With boundless energy, they scamper along the ground, their eyes fixed on the balloon like tiny adventurers chasing a floating dream. Excited waves and cheerful shouts rise up to you, carried by the gentle breeze. You can't help but wave to them, feeling an instant connection as you share in their unbridled joy.

The other balloon, vibrant and colorful, drifts gracefully against the gradually brightening blue sky. It gracefully moves in sync with the gentle breeze, sometimes gliding up or down or swaying vertically, adding to the enchanting scene.

You marvel at the world from above. The balloon operator shares that the journey is at the whim of the wind. There's no predetermined destination, only the path that the breeze takes you through the sky. This uncertainty isn't frightening. Rather, it's liberating. You embrace the scenery unfolding below, appreciating where the wind has taken you and the unique perspective it has offered.

The balloon's shadow, a dark, gentle giant, drifts across the fields below, a quiet companion on your journey. As the balloon floats on, the landscape changes. Below you are small villages, each with its own unique charm. Red-roofed houses cluster around ancient churches, their spires reaching up as if trying to touch your balloon. You glide over a small river that meanders near the town, its surface a shimmering ribbon in the morning sun.

The operator gently begins to lower the balloon, and you float over an open field of soft, green grass. Descending slowly, you can fully absorb the scene below. The simplicity of the landscape, with its subtle undulations and the occasional wildflower peeking through the green, invites a moment to cherish the view.

As the balloon touches down, the gentle bump brings you back to reality. The crew expertly secures the balloon, and you step out of the basket, feeling a sense of accomplishment and happiness. You thank the operator for this unforgettable experience.

Now it's time to leave. Come back to your body and to your present environment. Take this sense of peacefulness and wonder into your day or evening.

Journey 15: Paris

Inhale slowly, counting to three, filling your lungs with air. Exhale gently, counting to three, releasing any tension. Repeat this process, taking three deep, purposeful breaths, allowing your body to relax more deeply with each one.

Imagine setting off on a journey to Paris, the enchanting City of Light. It's a crisp autumn morning, perfect for exploring this historic city.

You arrive at your quaint boutique hotel, where the scent of fresh croissants wafts through the air, mingling with the subtle fragrance of freshly ground coffee. As you step into the courtyard, hints of lavender and rose from the carefully tended garden gently blend with the aroma, creating an inviting Parisian atmosphere. The hotel exudes classic French elegance, with its ornate furnishings and soft, warm lighting. Your room is cozy, and it boasts a window that offers a view of the Paris skyline. The bed, dressed in crisp, white linens, looks like it will provide you with a deeply restful sleep.

After settling into your room, you step out to explore the city. The streets of Paris, with their cobblestone paths and rows of charming cafés, beckon you to wander and discover. The gentle rustle of autumn leaves underfoot and the hum of the city create a soothing backdrop for your stroll.

As you meander through the city, you find yourself at the iconic Eiffel Tower. Standing beneath this structure, its grandeur and elegance strikes you. The intricate ironwork reaching for the sky is a sight to behold. A nearby tour guide tells a group that it is 1,083 feet tall, which is about 330 meters. You admire it, feeling a deep sense of awe for this emblem of Paris.

Continuing your journey, you walk along the Seine River. The water, flowing gently, reflects the soft autumn light. The sight of boats lazily drifting along, coupled with the picturesque bridges that span the river, adds to this scene. A duck swims by with its mate, and you admire this beautiful river and all the life along it.

Your path leads you to the charming district of Montmartre, which is a quaint, artistic area atop a hill in Paris, known for its cobbled streets. The soft sounds of a street musician playing a violin float through the air. You pass by several street vendors who are making crepes. The scent of sweet and savory delights surrounds you. After purchasing a crepe, you find the mix of flavors and textures truly exceptional. This culinary delight offers a moment of pure enjoyment amidst the bustling streets.

Eventually, you make your way to the Louvre Museum. The iconic glass pyramid in a courtyard creates a stunning contrast to the historic palace that houses the museum. The glass reflects the clouds above and you appreciate how nature's beauty is found in many places.

You decide to visit the museum. Venturing through its vast, echoing galleries, you hear your footsteps on the wooden floors. Turning a corner, you encounter the famous portrait of the Mona Lisa. Despite the throng of visitors, there is a quiet that pervades the room.

The Mona Lisa, smaller than you imagined, sits ensconced in her protective glass, her gaze following you as you traverse the room. Her smile, subtle yet profound, seems to hold some secrets. The rich, earthy tones of her attire and the backdrop of the painting contrast with the vibrancy of her eyes, which hold a depth that pierces.

After visiting the museum, you head over to the Tuileries Garden, which is close by. The garden, with its wide gravel paths, is filled with tourists and Parisians enjoying the sunny weather. You see families walking with small children, couples holding hands, and individuals like yourself who are appreciating the vibrant flowers. Dahlias, tulips, and roses live in a carefully tended garden along the pathway. You smell these floral scents as you take in the view of the many people along these large garden avenues.

You come upon serene ponds, cradled by manicured hedges, reflecting the clear sky above. Water lilies float on the water and remind you of Monet's paintings. The gentle murmur of water from the ornate fountains creates a soothing sound. You gaze at the beautiful water lilies with their white and pink flowers on top of the pond.

As you explore the gravel paths, your feet stir up a subtle, earthy aroma, grounding you in the moment. The touch of the breeze is gentle, which calms you. Occasional birds sing their songs, a reminder of the garden's role as a sanctuary not just for people, but for wildlife as well. The green benches, strategically placed under trees, offer a spot to sit and relax. You sit in the garden for a few minutes to rest before setting off to walk around Paris.

As evening approaches, you come upon a small French cafe on a side street, its inviting aromas wafting through the air. Inside, you're greeted by a cozy interior adorned with bright red chairs, and dimly lit by soft, warm lighting. The cafe offers an intimate atmosphere for you to savor some of your favorite dishes.

As the day draws to a close, the sun is setting as you walk across the iconic Pont Neuf, the oldest standing bridge across the Seine River. You pause in the middle of the bridge to see this breathtaking view. The river, a vein of life through the heart of the city, mirrors the sky's fading hues and the city's awakening lights. Historic buildings and bustling streets slowly exhibit twinkling lights. Streetlamps, buildings, and the vibrant glow from passing boats create a dynamic display of light, each shimmer reflecting off the gentle ripples of the Seine River.

Now it's time to leave Paris. Come back to your present environment and bring that feeling of wonder and peace into your day or evening.

Journey 16: Japanese Garden

Inhale slowly, counting to three, filling your lungs with air. Exhale gently, counting to three, releasing any tension. Repeat this process, taking three deep, purposeful breaths, allowing your body to relax more deeply with each one.

Imagine embarking on a journey in the fall to a sprawling Japanese garden. As you enter, a soft sandy pathway branches off in two directions. To your left stands a majestic red pagoda. The eaves of the pagoda curl upwards, their tips adorned with intricate gold accents that catch the sunlight, sparkling like jewels against the red. The wooden pillars display carvings of dragons, phoenixes, and other mythical creatures.

On your right, the path meanders around trees and flowering bushes. Drawn to the right, you find yourself alongside tall maple and aspen trees. Their branches form a lacework against the sky. Their leaves range from vibrant shades of red and orange to yellow and green. The trees form a lush covering overhead, with beams of sunlight piercing through, casting patterns of light on the ground, creating golden shapes at your feet.

Continuing along the path, you arrive at a large circular pond, home to koi fish. These graceful creatures, about a foot long, display an array of colors—vibrant oranges, striking whites, and deep blacks. They glide through the water with grace, their movements creating patterns that captivate your gaze. You stand there, letting your eyes relax into a soft focus, watching the fish swirl into a blur of orange and black, a visual meditation that soothes your mind.

An arched red wooden bridge, its curve forming a perfect semicircle, stands at the edge of the pond, offering a way to get across it. As you amble over the bridge, you catch sight of meticulously pruned rectangular bushes interspersed with camellias and chrysanthemums. The camellias, with their glossy, dark green leaves and rose-like flowers, range from deep crimson to light pink. Chrysanthemums unfurl their intricate petals in a variety of colors, from fiery reds to soft whites. The air is filled with a sweet, floral fragrance.

Once you cross the bridge, you stroll past the flowers and discover another section of the garden. There, you stumble upon a peaceful spot where you can appreciate breathtaking cherry trees in full bloom. Sitting under these trees on a flattened rock, you breathe in the air and admire the pink and white flowers that create a cloud-like effect around the tree. Each blossom has five small petals perched on a slender stem. You admire these wonders of nature.

Continuing your walk, you arrive at a quaint tea house, a modest square structure crafted from bamboo and wood. Inside, there are tatami mats on the floor. You marvel at the low ceiling, designed to foster a sense of humility, complemented by alcoves that display calligraphy. You've arrived just in time to witness a traditional Japanese tea ceremony. A person clad in a dark blue kimono kneels with grace, each movement deliberate and full of intent. They offer a respectful bow to the tea-making implements before expertly whisking bright green matcha powder into a frothy drink. After the ceremony, they invite you to taste the freshly prepared matcha, and you savor its earthy, rich flavors.

Your exploration continues as you come upon five bamboo fountains that vary in size. Each one gently drips water into a basin beneath, creating soothing, musical sounds. You breathe deeply and let the gentle sound of dripping water relax you.

Finally, you approach the large red pagoda that first caught your eye when you entered the garden. As the tallest structure, it exudes a sense of majesty and calm. As you enter the first floor, the gentle tinkle of wind chimes greets you, their melodies blending with the whisper of the breeze. Climbing several flights of stairs, you reach the topmost floor, where a view of the garden unfolds before you.

From this elevated vantage point, you can see the entire garden. The trees stretch out like a sea of green, red, yellow, and orange. You also see the cherry trees, the many flowers, and the serene pond. The winding paths, like ribbons, weave throughout.

You take your time at the top of the pagoda, allowing the peacefulness of the scene to wash over you. The rustling of the leaves, the distant sound of water, and the occasional chirp of a bird create appealing sounds. The few people walking within the garden add to this scene. A couple saunters slowly along the pathways as they point out different plants to each other. The air is fresh, filled with the subtle fragrance of the flowers and trees.

Reluctantly, you begin your descent from the top floor of the pagoda to the ground. Surrounding the pagoda, a meticulously crafted gravel walkway beckons you. This path winds around various plants and trees. The gentle crunch of gravel underfoot is a reminder of your connection with the surrounding environment.

You encounter a traditional stone lantern, its surface weathered by time, standing as a witness to the countless seasons that have passed. Moss and small ferns have made a home at its base, adding to its aged charm. You touch the stone surface and feel the softness of the moss.

Nearby stands a serene Buddha statue, carved from stone, exuding an aura of profound peace. The Buddha sits in a classic pose of meditation with eyes closed, hands gently folded in his lap. Over time, the elements have gently weathered the statue, so it blends seamlessly with the surrounding natural beauty. You touch the stone of the Buddha statue, feeling the cool, polished rock.

Now, it's time to leave the Japanese garden. Come back to your present environment and take this feeling of peacefulness into your day or evening.

Journey 17: Bicycling by the Lake

Inhale slowly, counting to three, filling your lungs with air. Exhale gently, counting to three, releasing any tension. Repeat this process, taking three deep, purposeful breaths, allowing your body to relax more deeply with each one.

Imagine going on a bicycle journey along a picturesque path that circles a deep blue lake during the early days of spring. You're greeted by a landscape slowly stirring from its winter slumber. On the left side, you can see trees with budding branches and small green leaves. To your right is the lake, which stretches out for several miles.

As you pedal, you feel a gentle breeze against your skin. The scent of grass, damp earth, and the fresh smell of the lake fill the air. You take a deep breath of these pleasant scents around you.

As you pedal along this lake path, the strength in your legs becomes clear, the steady push propelling you forward. Your bicycle moves in harmony with your body. Feel the push against the pedals, propelling your bicycle forward, then experience the effortless glide, especially on slight downward inclines.

You pass a cluster of weeping willow trees on your right that stand tall by the water's edge. Their slender branches, still bare from winter, sprout fresh green leaves, unfurling like delicate fingers reaching towards the ground. These willows, with their cascading foliage and gently swaying branches, mark the arrival of spring. A grand willow, the largest of the group, stands near the water and touches the lake's surface with its branches. You push against the pedals, moving quickly past these majestic trees.

In the distance lies a sandy area in front of the lake. The water glistens under the sun, its surface reflecting the sky above. A few fluffy white clouds hang overhead, adding to the picturesque view. On the far side of the lake are small mountains, their towering presence a stark contrast to the flat, inviting path you traverse.

When you reach the sandy area, you pause your ride to take a break. Dismounting, you stroll to the water's edge, finding some smooth stones along the shore. You feel the cool, polished surface of each stone, then toss them into the lake, listening to the satisfying plop or plunk as they hit the water. Some stones skip across the surface, each bounce creating ripples that expand in perfect circles until the stones finally vanish beneath the water.

You dip your fingers into the cool lake water, feeling the refreshing chill against your skin. After savoring these moments of calm by the water, you prepare to continue your ride. As you swing one leg over the bicycle, you see a bright red cardinal and its mate perched on a tree nearby. The male's vibrant red feathers stand out while its companion displays a subtle beauty with feathers of muted brown, subtly tinged with hues of red. Its trilling song, a series of high-pitched 'what cheer' calls, fills the air, adding to your experience. You admire these beautiful creatures.

Resuming your ride, you follow the path to the other side of the lake, where it weaves between two small mountains and ascends. Your energy surges as you tackle the uphill climb. The path zigzags up the mountainside, each turn offering a new view of the lake and its surroundings. The climb is challenging. As you tackle each upward curve, your legs exert more force on the pedals, causing you to sweat under the combination of the sunshine and your exertion. Reaching a high point, you pause to catch your breath, taking in the expansive view. The lake waters below shimmer.

After a brief rest and a refreshing drink of water, you begin the descent. The switchbacks carved into the mountain's side make for an exhilarating ride. You control your speed with occasional braking, relishing the effortless glide after your strenuous climb. With each turn, you come closer to the lake, the view changes, and you appreciate the cool breeze against your skin.

Now at the mountain's base, you follow the path you rode earlier, making your way back to the sandy area of the lakeshore. A gentle breeze stirs small waves that softly lap against the shore, creating a rhythmic sound. Dismounting from your bike, you stand at the water's edge, enjoying the sight of the ripples gliding over the lake's surface.

A family of geese glides gracefully across the water. A large goose, with its proud posture and sleek feathers, leads the way, guiding its mate and goslings in a neat formation behind it. The adults' feathers shine in the sunlight, displaying a rich combination of earthy browns, creamy whites, and subtle grays. Their long necks arch gracefully, and their bright eyes scan the surroundings. They glimpse at you and continue.

The awkward goslings paddle close to their parents. Their downy feathers carry traces of soft, yellow fluff. They emit soft peeping sounds as they follow, occasionally darting ahead before quickly returning to the group.

The adults make occasional honking noises, which reverberate across the water. Watching the family of geese glide along the lake, you marvel at this sweet family and how connected they are to one another.

You get back on your bicycle, feeling reinvigorated and ready to continue your ride. The path leads you to a section of the lake where you find a weathered dock with a simple wooden rowboat. The boat bobs gently in the water, rising and falling with the motion of the lake, as if eager to set sail once more.

It's time to leave the lake. Come back to your present environment. Come back to your body, feeling your fingers and toes. Take this feeling of contentment with you into your day or evening.

Journey 18: Ancient Library

Inhale slowly, counting to three, filling your lungs with air. Exhale gently, counting to three, releasing any tension. Repeat this process, taking three deep, purposeful breaths, allowing your body to relax more deeply with each one.

Imagine you are going to visit an ancient library. It's housed in an enormous stone building that has been used for several hundred years. Ancient scholars have used it for centuries.

As you approach the massive, ornately carved oak doors of the library, a sense of awe comes over you. You pull on the heavy doors, which creak open, stepping into the cool, dimly lit interior. The air is heavy with the scent of aged parchment, leather-bound books, and the subtle aroma of polished wood.

Before you, a vast hall stretches out with regal elegance. A soaring arched ceiling above you reminds you of a cathedral. In the heart of this great room, sit rows of wooden study tables. About fifty of them are arranged in two long rows. The soft glow of lamps illuminates the polished wood as people sit studiously. The only sound you hear is the occasional rustle of pages and sometimes a whisper. This is a silent place.

You stand on a floor made of polished wooden planks, which reflects the warm light streaming in from the tall windows near the arched ceiling. You wonder how many people have walked on these floors over the years.

Two extensive floors of bookshelves rise on the left and right of these study tables. Each level holds many alcoves where countless volumes rest. Every alcove offers a secluded haven, complete with its own reading space. You explore several archives on the first floor before deciding you want to visit the second level.

You ascend to the second floor by climbing a wide wooden staircase at the end of this gigantic building. Feeling the large, polished oak banister, you climb the grand stairs toward the vaulted ceiling. From this elevated place, you see the study tables below and the golden sunlight on the wooden floor.

You walk along one of the many aisles of the second floor. The towering shelves on either side are filled with books of all sizes and shapes, some with spines embossed with gold and intricate designs. Reaching out, your fingers trace the textures of the bindings, feeling the embossed patterns and the smoothness of the leather, connecting you with the craftsmanship of these volumes.

One book with a red spine captures your attention. Unlike the thicker volumes nearby, this one is slender, its bright red color stands out vividly against the muted tones of its neighbors. Drawing it from its place, you feel an immediate connection, as if this book was waiting just for you, its pages ready to tell stories you would appreciate.

As you begin reading, the book invites you into a narrative so interesting that the world around you fades away. You sink into a chair nestled in a cozy nook of the library, the light of a reading lamp casting a warm glow over the book in your hands. Feel the softness of the chair, the way it cradles your body, and realize you have nowhere you need to go. You can enjoy this lovely moment.

The story begins in a small village known as Eldridge Hollow, which lies at the edge of a vast forest. The village is described so clearly that you see hues of emerald green and earthen browns in your mind. You can smell the fresh, pine-scented air and feel the wind that rustles through the leaves, carrying whispers of ancient secrets.

The main character is a young woman named Elizabeth, whose spirit is as wild and untamed as the forest that borders her home. With hair as black as the midnight sky and eyes equally dark, Elizabeth has an innate connection to the natural world. Her dreams contain visions of places beyond her home, of mysteries that reveal themselves in cryptic ways.

Elizabeth's life takes a dramatic turn when she discovers a journal hidden in the attic of her family's cottage. The journal belonged to her grandmother, a renowned explorer and guardian of the village's lore. Through the carefully penned entries, Elizabeth learns of an ancient relic believed to hold the power to protect or doom her village. The relic, known as the Heart of the Forest, was lost decades ago in the woods.

Driven by a sense of destiny and the burning desire to protect her village, Elizabeth sets out on a journey into the forest. Each step takes her deeper into a world of enchantment and peril. The forest is alive, with whispering trees that guide or mislead, hidden springs with waters that heal or harm, and creatures that walk the line between animal and spirit.

As Elizabeth's journey unfolds, you walk alongside her, feeling the uneven ground beneath her feet and the thorns that snag at her clothes. You wonder if the fairy that appears is good or evil, and if Elizabeth should take the elixir offered. You hope that as she traverses the small river that the evil sprite doesn't catch her, transforming her into a moss-covered rock by the water. This fate has happened to others who have trod this path.

The climax of the tale arrives in a clearing lit by moonlight, where an ancient and formidable spirit guards the Heart of the Forest itself. Elizabeth engages in a fierce battle using a magic sword and saves Eldridge Hollow.

Emerging from the story, you find yourself back in the ancient library, holding the bright red book.

Now it's time to leave the library. Slowly, bring your awareness back to your current surroundings, carrying with you these feelings of wonder and contentment into your day or evening.

Journey 19: Apple Orchard

Inhale slowly, counting to three, filling your lungs with air. Exhale gently, counting to three, releasing any tension. Repeat this process, taking three deep, purposeful breaths, allowing your body to relax more deeply with each one.

Imagine yourself within a sprawling apple orchard during the vibrant autumn season, when it's time for apple-picking. The orchard presents a dazzling sight, with rows and rows of apples in various shades. From deep burgundy and cheerful yellow to bright green, the orchard offers a rich palette of colors.

Today presents the perfect opportunity to meander among the many apple trees. The ground beneath your feet feels soft, and you notice the occasional apple that has tumbled from the branches above. Natural paths weave between the trees, hinting at the passage of those who have wandered these rows before you, harvesting the fruit.

The trees stand in neat rows, their branches heavy, some bending under the weight of apples. Bright sunlight floods the orchard, accentuating the beauty of the trees. The air is tinged with the sweet, tangy scent of ripe apples. You breathe in this fresh air and the scent of the many apples around you.

As you amble along, you notice how the apples hanging from the branches capture the sunlight, making them appear to glow with an inner light. Their skin is smooth and glossy. They vary in shape and size—some appear perfectly round and plump, while others boast quirky twists and turns, each one a testament to life's diversity.

The orchard comes alive with the rustling of leaves as the breeze dances through the trees. You listen to the gentle sound of the leaves brushing against one another and feel the sun on your face.

You also hear the songs of birds flitting around the orchard. Occasionally you see a movement where you think a bird landed, but mostly you hear them. Their melodies, a mixture of chirps, tweets, and trills, weave through the trees. These birds are attracted by the insects and probably some of the ripe apples.

Nearby, an apple dislodges from its branch and falls to the ground with a soft plunk, a common occurrence in this landscape. You can't help but wonder about the quiet drama of apples falling unnoticed throughout the day.

Among the trees, a small wooden bench offers a place for rest and reflection. Seated here, you take in the orchard with its many trees, large variety of apples, and the birds nearby.

You are drawn to a large apple tree, its branches heavy with ripe fruit. Approaching the tree, you select a perfect apple, its skin smooth and flushed with color. You begin to pull it from the branch. At first the tree resists, but with a gentle tug it releases the fruit into your hand.

As you hold the apple, you feel the smoothness of its skin beneath your fingertips. Notice the slight coolness. You rotate the apple in your hand, observing the subtle variations in its texture and the different colors on its skin. Each color blends into the next.

You bring the apple closer and examine its stem. This was once its lifeline to the tree. As you feel the stem with your fingertips, you admire what nature has created. The gentle curve of the apple fits so naturally in the palm of your hand. You feel the weight and size of this fruit.

You marvel at this apple and then take a bite. The fruit is crisp and juicy, bursting with sweetness and a hint of tartness that delights the palate. The flavor is rich and complex, a reflection of the soil, sunlight, and care that has nurtured it to ripeness.

As you savor the apple, the flavors and textures invite you to be fully present. Feel the texture and taste of the skin, the interior of this fruit, and how it blends in your mouth. The act of eating the apple becomes a meditation in itself—a celebration of the senses and the simple yet profound joys that nature offers.

You finish your apple and then sit, enjoying the moment. The beauty of the orchard, the trees arranged in rows, the varied colors of the apples, and the crisp air around you.

As you appreciate the orchard, a movement catches your eye—a brown sparrow has landed on the ground nearby, its attention captivated by a fallen, ripe apple. The sparrow hops closer to the fruit with cautious curiosity, its tiny feet lightly treading on the soft ground. With delicate movements, it pecks at the apple, taking small nibbles.

A gentle breeze rustles through the orchard, causing the sparrow to pause mid-peck. With a quick flutter of its wings, the bird takes flight, disappearing among the fruit trees.

As you sit there, a robin with a bright red breast lands gracefully on a low-hanging branch nearby. The robin glances at you and then tilts its head to the side as it surveys the fallen apple below. With a cheerful chirp, the robin hops close to the fruit and begins feasting on it.

As you sit quietly, you notice a delicate ladybug meandering along a slender branch. Its vibrant red shell, covered with tiny black spots, showcases the many forms of natural beauty.

With gentle and deliberate movements, the ladybug explores its leafy terrain, its tiny legs delicately gripping the surface with each step. Its translucent wings are tucked neatly beneath its shell, ready to unfold at a moment's notice should the need to take flight arise.

Now, it's time to leave the orchard. Bring your awareness back to your current environment, carrying with you the orchard's peacefulness and wonder into your day or evening.

Journey 20: European Village

Inhale slowly, counting to three, filling your lungs with air. Exhale gently, counting to three, releasing any tension. Repeat this process, taking three deep, purposeful breaths, allowing your body to relax more deeply with each one.

Imagine embarking on a journey to a quaint, rural European village. It's late spring, the perfect time to experience the European countryside. You stay in a charming hotel, nestled in the heart of the village, that hosts only a few guests. It's an ideal escape from everyday life.

After checking into your hotel, you set out to explore the village. You're captivated by the small beige stucco houses adorned with brightly colored windows and doors. Some boast vibrant blue doors and shutters, while others feature striking emerald green or bold crimson, standing out vividly against the backdrop of the clear blue sky.

The angular roofs of the houses have slate or terracotta tiles, adding to the rustic allure of the village. Hanging from many windows are planters overflowing with flowers such as geraniums, petunias, and marigolds. You inhale the fragrances of these flowers as you admire these brightly colored homes.

You walk through the small streets, feeling the cobblestones underfoot, which are uneven and worn smooth by the passage of many people. Your steps take you to the heart of the village—the town square, which has small shops surrounding a magnificent fountain.

You head over to the flowing fountain, which features a statue of an enormous fish at the highest tier. The sculptor intricately carved the scales and gills of the fish statue to reveal its beauty. Water joyously spills from the fish's open mouth, cascading down to an assembly of creatures—frogs, water birds, and smaller fish below. The artist carved these creatures with such precision that they seem alive. They almost seem to dance within this aquatic haven as they receive a gentle spray of water.

At the base, the main pool of the fountain is a wide, circular basin, its center a frothy display of water as it drops from above. Sunlight plays upon the water's surface, creating glints of light that appear and disappear as the water moves. Coins shine on the basin's bottom, thrown by wishful villagers and visitors alike. You admire this fountain and watch the water as it splashes into the large basin. Listen to the soothing sounds.

The air is fragrant with the aroma of fresh bread and pastries coming from the open door of a bakery on the town square. A small bell chimes as someone exits, and you catch the scent of yeast and flour, a smell that promises warmth and comfort. A few doors down, a local cafe spills out onto the street, its tables under the shade of a leafy tree. The murmur of conversation mingles with the clink of coffee cups, providing you with an invitation to pause and soak in the sounds of village life.

Everywhere you look, the village is alive. A narrow alleyway off the square comes alive with the sounds of children's laughter. A group of kids chase each other, their games echoing off the ancient stone walls that have seen generations of play. The air resonates with their joyous shouts and the thud of a well-loved ball bouncing on the cobblestones.

Nearby, under the shade of a vine-covered trellis, a person sits reading a newspaper. Their glasses perch on the bridge of their nose as they read, absorbed in the stories of the wider world. A plump orange cat lounges nearby in a sunbeam, its fur a patchwork of light and shadow.

Further into the square, a young couple meanders by, their hands entwined. They move as if they are in their own private bubble, oblivious to the world around them. Their murmurs and shared glances speak volumes.

The town center is a mosaic of life. Market stalls on one side of the square overflow with fruits and vegetables in an array of vibrant colors. Artisanal jams, jellies, and soaps hint at the time-honored traditions behind their creation. The air is thick with the scents of ripe produce, fragrant blooms, and the aroma of freshly baked bread from the nearby bakery. You pause to breathe in these fragrances and to admire these market stalls.

You continue walking, and as the day wanes and evening approaches, the setting sun casts a golden light over the village. The colors of the houses deepen, becoming richer and more intense, while the shadows lengthen on the cobblestone streets. Within the small homes, lights flicker on, creating warm interiors.

You return to the hotel for dinner. The soft glow of the fireplace and plush armchairs adds to the inviting atmosphere of the sitting room. With its wooden beams and softly lit candles, the dining room exudes rustic charm. The air is filled with the comforting scent of home-cooked food, promising a delicious meal.

After dinner, you take a leisurely stroll through the village, now quiet under the starry sky. Some stars gleam with a bright, steady radiance, casting gentle rays of light across the darkness. Others twinkle more faintly, like distant jewels. The sky is a deep, velvety blue with the occasional gray cloud above. As you admire the view, a shooting star streaks across the sky, leaving a fleeting trail of light in its wake. It's a sight that fills you with a sense of awe and wonder.

Now it's time to leave this village. Come back to the present environment and take these peaceful feelings into your day or evening.

Journey 21: Autumn Walk

Take a deep breath and count to three, feeling the air expand your lungs. Exhale gently, counting to three, releasing any tension. Continue taking three deep, mindful breaths, each exhale helping you to sink deeper into a state of relaxation.

Imagine visiting a large public park on a crisp fall day. Ahead, a broad pathway stretches out, lined by trees that have responded to the fall weather, their leaves transforming into a vibrant array of colors. As you walk beneath the trees, the sight of orange, yellow, red, and green leaves create a stunning vista. Some leaves have fallen, and they create a patchwork of colors along the ground. You take in this beautiful scene of trees displaying their many colors along this wide path.

As you walk along, you feel the crunch of leaves under your feet. Two children race ahead of you, one playfully chasing the other. Around you, people stroll along, basking in the scenery, engaged in animated conversations. A group of friends tell jokes to one another, and they laugh uproariously at the punchline.

Seeing a bright orange maple leaf on the ground, you pick it up. Your finger traces the veins of this leaf. It's a tremendous creation with many colors. Although the predominant hue is orange, it also has spots of yellow and a few flecks of red. It's soft and fragile. A reminder of how everything changes, how each leaf tells a story of growth, transformation, and ultimately, renewal.

The path gently leads you to the tranquil edge of a small pond. Here, brown wooden benches, weathered yet welcoming, offer a place to sit. You choose one and settle into a moment of quiet observation of the water.

Large stones encircle the pond, creating a walkway for ducks and other small creatures. Each stone, unique in its contours and placement, seems to tell its own story of time's passage. Some rest heavily on the earth, having sunk into the soft ground beneath the weight of years, while others lay sprawled, their broad backs offering a resting place for the light. The stones vary in color, from the palest silver to the deepest gray.

The light green pond hints at its shallow depths, with pebbles and water plants visible near the edges. In the center of the pond lies a modest island, home to several Mallard ducks. Tall grasses encircle the island, creating a boundary between water and land.

Some parts of the island rise slightly higher, providing vantage points for the ducks to survey their surroundings.

The Mallard ducks, recognizable by the males' iridescent green heads and bright orange bills, add vibrant splashes of color to the scene. Amidst the tall grasses, you occasionally see the ducks disappearing into concealed areas, suggesting hidden nesting spots where they weave together reeds and grasses to create cozy shelters for their eggs. As they glide gracefully across the water or waddle along the island's edge, their occasional quacks and playful interactions enliven the atmosphere, reminding you of the rich diversity of wildlife that thrives in this natural habitat.

A family with two young children wanders over and sits on a nearby bench. The children are identical twins who are probably four or five years old. Their parents give them something they're enjoying, and you see wide smiles and eager requests for more. The simple joy of family, of sharing moments and treats, fills you with warmth.

A duck floats in front of you, followed by several small ducklings who form a perfect line. You marvel at seeing their little webbed feet paddling beneath the surface. As they swim away, you see a trail of water behind them, ripples spreading out and reaching the shore, creating an enchanting pattern in the water. These ripples, ever-expanding, remind you of the impact of small actions, the beauty in the wake we leave behind.

You take a deep breath, savoring the freshness of the air, tinged with the unmistakable scent of the pond and fallen leaves. These earthy aromas are the essence of autumn.

Eventually, you take a path away from the pond to a cluster of deep green bushes. Someone has meticulously pruned them into geometric shapes. In the center stands a large circular bush, surrounded by a ring of individual bushes. One bush is triangular, another is square, and yet another is rectangular. This geometric bush garden is delightful, and you imagine someone lovingly tending to it regularly. It's a testament to the human ability to shape and coexist with nature.

Now the path leads you to another cluster of trees. Among them stands the largest, its massive trunk and twisted branches stretching skyward, with a mix of green and yellow leaves. Beneath its expansive canopy, scattered yellow leaves lie in various stages of transition. Some have recently fallen, while others, brittle and dry, have rested on the ground for some time.

You reach out and touch the rough bark of the tree, tracing your fingers along its surface. The wide girth of its trunk and the texture of its bark hint at its age, indicating that this is indeed an old tree. You admire this majestic tree, which is a reminder of the enduring strength and resilience inherent in the natural world.

As you stand beneath the towering tree, you notice movement out of the corner of your eye. A playful gray squirrel scampers over, its bushy tail flicking with excitement as it races up the trunk of the tree. Pausing for a moment, the squirrel peers down at you with curiosity, its bright eyes filled with a sense of wonder. You can't help but smile at the tiny visitor, feeling a sense of connection to this place as you share this moment with one of its inhabitants.

Now it's time to leave this beautiful park. Come back to your current environment and take this feeling of tranquility into your day or evening.

Journey 22: Caribbean Island

Inhale slowly, counting to three, filling your lungs with air. Exhale gently, counting to three, releasing any tension. Repeat this process, taking three deep, purposeful breaths, allowing your body to relax more deeply with each one.

Imagine visiting a small, secluded Caribbean Island. This is a resort that allows only a few guests each year. This is a private and exclusive experience.

As you step into your opulent suite, its luxury and comfort impress you. The suite has two exquisitely appointed bedrooms, each adorned with plush linens. In the living room, plush couches and overstuffed chairs tempt you to sink into them. As you take in the exquisite furnishings, you can't help but gaze at the walls adorned with Caribbean-inspired artwork, with each piece reminding you of the beauty of this island.

Next to the living room, the dining area beckons with a polished table set against a backdrop of floor-to-ceiling windows that offer panoramic views of the turquoise waters beyond. Here, you can indulge in gourmet meals prepared by the resort's world-class chefs. But perhaps the most enchanting feature of the suite is its covered porch. Here, you can recline in comfortable lounge chairs, sip on tropical cocktails, and listen to the ocean.

During the midday hours, you visit the resort's restaurant. You choose a table in the outside dining area, where you hear the ocean's waves rolling onto the shore. You can see a few people on the beach engaged in various activities. Some are basking in the sun, others are engrossed in their books, and a few are frolicking in the surf, which breaks a few yards away. The ocean stretches out before you with vibrant blue-green colors near the shoreline, transforming to soft, light blues, and then a deep navy further out. This ever-changing seascape and the people along the beach absorb your attention.

After finishing your meal, the server tells you about the various paths around the island, each leading to different beaches. You set off along a palm-lined path, the fronds rustling softly in the gentle breeze. The first beach you encounter, Harmony Beach, is small and secluded. Coconuts dot the sand, and a large, rusted key, washed ashore, catches your eye. Curious, you pick up the key, pondering its mysterious origins. Feel the heft of this key in your hands.

As you walk along, your imagination runs wild with the idea that the key could unlock a chest of sunken pirate treasures. You chuckle to yourself, entertained by the fanciful thought, which adds lightness to your steps.

The next beach along the path is larger, and here you see a small family enjoying the sand and sea. One parent reads a book, looks up, and smiles warmly at you. The other adult plays with a small child in the sand, their laughter ringing out as they dig an immense hole. The scene is heartwarming, a reminder of the simple joys of life.

Leaving the family behind, you continue your walk. As you approach the third beach, you notice the path narrowing, surrounded by dense trees. The beach's seclusion adds to its allure, and you feel as if you've stumbled on a secret paradise. The shade from the trees provides a cool respite from the sun, and the sound of waves crashing against the shore is louder, more pronounced here. You enjoy the scent of the sea water along with the view of waves coming and leaving the shore, leaving a wet trace behind each time.

As you explore, you discover hidden coves along the beach. In one cove, you find a starfish nestled in a tidal pool. It rests on the sandy bottom, its arms spread in perfect symmetry. Its color is a mesmerizing hue of deep orange, with hints of pink at the tips of its arms. The starfish's body appears both rugged and delicate, dotted with tiny protrusions. You marvel at how life occurs in so many forms on this earth.

As the sun begins its descent towards the horizon, a soft golden light transforms the beach, gently touching everything. The waves, rolling gently onto the shore, catch the sun's rays, creating sparkling paths of light across the water's surface. Each wave glitters.

In the distance, seabirds glide gracefully against the glowing sky. Along the shoreline, a sandpiper emerges, a small and slender bird that dips and weaves as it scuttles across the sand. Its brown feathers resemble the color of sand, providing excellent camouflage along the beach. With quick and agile movements, it darts forward with lightning-fast precision in search of food. You notice its thin legs, perfectly adapted for navigating the sandy shoreline. Pausing momentarily, it stretches its wings, revealing flashes of white on its underside.

Slowly, you make your way back to the resort as the sun sets. You wander back through the two beaches, passing the family packing up their belongings. The child waves and smiles at you.

You return to your luxurious suite and have a delightful dinner while you watch the sun's descent into the ocean from your dining room. After dinner, you sit on the porch, relaxing as the full moon lights up the sky. The moonlight dances across the waves, creating a path of light that seems to lead directly to your resort. The ocean takes on a mysterious depth, with areas darkening under the moon's watchful eye. Your mind wanders to the intriguing discovery of the large old key earlier in the day, and you envision a sunken ship with a treasure chest somewhere out there on the bottom of the ocean.

Retiring to your bed, you fall asleep to the lullaby of waves washing onto the beach. The rhythmic sound lulls you into a deep, restful sleep.

Now it's time to leave this island. Come back to your present environment and bring this feeling of tranquility into your day or evening.

Journey 23: Secret Garden

Inhale slowly, counting to three, feeling the air expand your lungs. Exhale gently, counting to three, releasing any tension. Continue this rhythm, taking three deep, mindful breaths, each exhale helping you to sink deeper into a state of relaxation.

Imagine a journey along a path in a forest known for its vibrant wildlife. The air is alive with birds chirping and calling to each other, creating a backdrop of natural sounds. As you amble forward, a monarch butterfly, with its striking orange and black pattern, flutters across your path before landing on a flowering bush. You watch as it delicately opens and closes its wings, visiting several white blossoms. The flowers create a stark contrast to the butterfly's intense colors.

Further along the path, you encounter a tall, rusty wrought-iron gate. Its weathered appearance hints at its age, yet its structure stands firm. It beckons you forward, its silent invitation stirring a sense of curiosity. You step through the gate, crunching sticks on the ground. The sunlight bathes the path ahead in a bright glow, highlighting the lush greenery along the trail and the majestic trees around you.

As you tread along the forest path, a flash of color catches your eye. A blue jay perches on a nearby branch, its feathers a stunning array of lighter and deeper blues. Accentuating its colorful feathers are patches of crisp white framing its wings and tail. You hear its distinctive cry, ranging from high-pitched squawks to melodic trills. The blue jay alights from its perch and heads into the forest, flying along the path ahead.

You follow the blue jay, noticing how it lands intermittently on low-hanging branches along the trail. Some of its feathers sparkle with hints of purple, while others take on a dark, almost black color. Towards the lower half of its body, square designs adorn its feathers, giving it the appearance of wearing a miniature quilt. The triangular blue crown of this creature exudes majesty, perhaps the reason it is considered so regal.

Eventually, the blue jay leads you to a charming clearing. Here, a wild garden thrives with a gentle disorder, bursting with an array of flowers. Around you are clusters of wild roses, hyacinths, gardenias, and yellow black-eyed Susans. It seems like nobody has tended to the clearing in a long time.

At the heart of this wild garden, a gray gravel pathway leads to a striking fountain. A statue of a dark green mermaid appears ready to dive into unseen depths, with a dolphin by her side. Water jets from the fountain's center, cascading over the pair in a sparkling shower, bring the scene to life. The mermaid and dolphin, caught in a moment of frozen motion, possess an otherworldly charm, as if they might spring to life and vanish beneath the waves at any moment, leaving behind their secret garden.

You meander along the gravel pathway, each step marked by a crunch beneath your feet, drawing you closer to the statue. With every step, your walk becomes more measured, more deliberate, allowing a wave of relaxation to wash over you. As you come closer to the fountain, the mermaid statue commands your attention, its presence larger than life. Water bursts forth from behind the figure, draping over her shoulders before cascading gracefully down her fishtail and gently enveloping her dolphin friend.

You touch the fountain's water, finding it surprisingly warm against your skin. The water's gentle flow through your fingers feels soothing, prompting you to immerse your other hand as well, basking in this warm sensation.

The statue showcases exceptional craftsmanship. When the sunlight catches the scales on her tail, it glimmers with a lifelike quality. Her face exudes an expression of serenity. You can envision her joyfully frolicking in the ocean with her dolphin companion, exploring sunken wrecks with excitement. As the sun sets, you can imagine her gracefully returning to her underwater castle, disappearing into the depths as the light fades. You search for a title, or the name of the sculptor associated with the statue, but find nothing.

As you move around the fountain looking at the statue from different angles, the sound of water is a constant, calming presence. The gentle splashing is a soothing sound.

You take a seat on a nearby bench, made of intricately carved stone. It's cool and solid beneath you. From here, you can see the entire clearing, encircled by tall trees that stand as sentries of this place. Wild roses with their delicate petals in shades of soft pink, subtly perfume the air. Nearby, clusters of hyacinths offer a striking contrast with their dense spikes of blossoms and soft purple color.

Nearby, some yellow black-eyed Susans stand out with their dark brown centers surrounded by golden petals. Gardenias, with creamy white velvety petals, seem to glow against the dark green foliage. The wild and unkempt nature of this garden enhances its allure—it's thriving on its own terms.

In some areas, the unexpected pop of color catches your eye. Lavender sprigs with their delicate, slender flowers seem to beckon to you. Their rich fragrance wafts through the air. You approach the lavender and breathe in this calming scent.

As you leave the garden, you take another look at the mermaid statue with her dolphin friend. You wonder how many people have found this secret garden as you take the pathway back into the forest and walk through the wrought-iron gate. As you squeeze past the gate, you see a blue jay in the distance. Nature is truly wondrous.

Now it's time to leave this forest. Come back to your present environment and bring this feeling of peace into your day or evening.

Journey 24: Evening Sail

Inhale slowly, counting to three, feeling the air fill your lungs. Exhale gently, counting to three, releasing any tension. Repeat this process, taking three deep, purposeful breaths, allowing your body to relax more deeply with each one.

Imagine standing on the soft sand of a beach. The sun hovers just above the horizon, casting a warm, golden light that dances across the surface of the sea. You hear the waves lapping against the shore, and the distant call of seabirds bidding the day farewell. A gentle breeze brushes against you. It's a perfect evening for sailing.

You make your way to a lengthy deck that extends outward from the shoreline, leading to where a sailboat awaits. Its sleek, elegant white hull rests gracefully on the water's surface, swaying softly with the gentle waves. A sailor greets you warmly, welcoming you aboard. As you step onto the vessel, you notice the sturdy wooden deck underfoot. Every surface of the craft, including the deck, railing, floors, benches, and doors, features polished wood that glistens like amber. You run your hands along the smooth wood of the railing, feeling the craftsmanship and care that created it.

The time has come to set sail. With a sense of ceremony, the sailor unfurls the sails, catching the evening breeze. The boat responds immediately, gliding forward with a gentle grace from the wind propelling it. By adjusting the position of the sails, the sailor guides the vessel away from the shore.

Water extends to the horizon, creating a boundless expanse of glistening blue that blends with the sky at the world's edge. The sun, now a deep orange, sinks lower, painting the sky in hues of yellow, rich marmalade, and amber. This spectacle of color reflects on the water's surface. You take in the sky's beauty and its reflection on the surrounding water.

As you sail further from the shore, the vibrant life beneath the waves occasionally reveals itself. Schools of fish dart just below the surface, their silvery bodies glinting in the light, a fleeting glimpse into the teeming world beneath the sea. Every so often, you hear a fish leaping from the water and see the ripples that are left behind after it returns to its world.

In the distance, the silhouette of a lighthouse appears, standing guard on a rocky promontory that extends into the sea. Its bold red stripes that spiral from top to bottom remind you of a gigantic candy cane. This structure, perched on top of boulders, evokes images of a bygone era, safeguarding mariners against the treacherous coast. You wonder whether it still serves as a beacon for modern vessels navigating these waters. The exterior looks as if it was recently painted, which suggests this is a working lighthouse.

As the journey continues, the outline of a distant island slowly emerges. Its shape becomes clearer as you sail nearer. Bathed in the soft glow of the fading light, the island reveals rugged cliffs and pristine beaches. The island's interior is a lush expanse of dense foliage, where towering trees rise high into the sky, creating a wilderness that appears untouched by humans.

At dusk, the tranquility of the sea is soothing. The whisper of the wind in the sails, the gentle creaking of the boat as it carves its path through the water, and the recurring splash of waves against the hull. As the boat glides through the water, you hear these soothing sounds and feel increasingly relaxed.

The air becomes cool, and you put on a warm jacket. You take a deep breath of the clean, salty sea air mixed with the subtle smell of the sailcloth and the wood of the boat. These scents connect you to this moment.

As the sun finally slips below the edge of the world, the blue sky transforms into a spectrum of twilight colors, where shades of deep blue and velvety purple intermingle. It's as if an enormous artist has painted the sky with gigantic brushes right in front of you. As the minutes pass, the intensity of these colors deepens. The fading light dances upon the clouds, turning them into wisps of rose and gold, as if bidding a fond farewell to the departing sun.

Meanwhile, the sea shifts with the changing light. The waters, once a clear, sunlit blue, transform into deeper shades of teal and purple. The surface of the sea, textured by gentle waves and soft ripples, captures the last rays of sunlight glimmering at the crests of small waves.

This gradual dimming of the light sets the stage for the night sky. Stars emerge, just pinpricks of light. Against this backdrop, the moon appears, ascending gradually, its silvery light growing in intensity. It casts a serene glow across the sea's surface, illuminating the waters with a path of light. You admire this moonlight across the water and see it reflected in the gentle waves.

As you relax, you notice tiny specks of light twinkling like stars under the water. Intrigued, you lean over the side of the boat. The water appears alive with a mesmerizing glow, as if a thousand tiny fairies are dancing beneath the surface. According to the sailor, these are bioluminescent plankton—microscopic organisms that generate their own light. They emit pulses of soft blue-green light, creating an enchanting underwater world. With each gentle movement of the waves, the twinkling lights intensify, casting a delightful glow that illuminates the surrounding sea.

The endless expanse of sea and sky, the gentle rocking of the boat, the beauty of the plankton, and the soft glow of the moon create a sense of timelessness. You take one last breath of sea air as you enjoy this wonderful experience.

Now it's time to leave this sailing adventure. Come back to your present environment and bring this sense of wonder and peacefulness into your day or evening.

Journey 25: Mountain Retreat

Inhale slowly, counting to three, filling your lungs with air. Exhale gently, counting to three, releasing any tension. Repeat this process, taking three deep, purposeful breaths, allowing your body to relax more deeply with each one.

Imagine standing at the edge of a vast forest that blankets the foothills of an imposing mountain range. It's a cool spring day. The surrounding air is alive with the scent of pine and the earthy aroma of damp soil. A path lays ahead of you that will bring you up the mountain.

As you begin your journey, you admire the towering pine trees standing on either side of the path, their boughs swaying in the wind as if they're dancing. Sticks and twigs lie along the route, and you notice large trees that have fallen long ago, covered in moss and other vegetation. Sunlight filters through the dense covering, dappling the forest floor in patches of light.

Feel the climb in your legs as you slowly ascend this mountain. Your energy is powerful, and you feel invigorated as you follow the pathway that many have already trod. You stop every so often to take a drink of cool water you've brought along for your trip.

As you reach a higher elevation, a clearing in the trees offers you a stunning view of the mountainside. Looking downward, you see the forest of trees clinging to the steep slopes, a lush expanse of green that stretches as far as you can see. These trees, in various shades of emerald and jade, create a beautiful tapestry of natural colors. Among them, taller trees rise prominently, their thick trunks and broad canopies make them appear as if they're watching over the younger, smaller trees.

Your gaze follows the mountain's descent to the valley floor, where a wide river carves its path at the bottom. This lively waterway is a ribbon of blue, its waters rushing and tumbling over rocks. In areas where the sun shines on the water, it appears a sparkling blue. And in the shadowed bends and deeper areas, it adopts a deeper color. When the river's current meets the rugged obstacles in its path, white foam appears against the liquid blue.

Beyond the river, the land begins its ascent once more, rising to form another mountain that mirrors the one on which you stand. This opposite slope climbs from the valley, its rise marked by the gradual retreat of the forest into the rugged, bare rock with low shrubbery at higher points.

After sipping your cool drink, you continue to climb. Further up the path, you enter a clearing and find a small mountain lake nestled among the trees. The water is crystal clear. You sit by the lake's edge and dip your hands in, feeling the cool, clean water.

An enormous old pine tree stands nearby, its gnarled roots clinging to the mountain soil, its branches reaching skyward. You lean against its sturdy trunk, feeling the rough texture of its bark against your back, and look up to see the sunlight through its needles.

After a while, you carry on with your journey and come upon a large cabin. Nestled among the trees, this building is crafted from weathered wood, seamlessly blending into its natural surroundings. In front of the cabin, a gentle stream murmurs as it cascades over rocks. The cabin appears quite spacious, and you envision it containing many rooms. You admire the skillful assembly of the dark brown logs, the wisps of smoke curling from the chimney, and the inviting porch that calls out, urging you to take a seat and unwind.

As you approach the cabin, a door opens with a gentle creak, and a person welcomes you, explaining the cabin is a place to relax and recover. It's available for all hikers who traverse this trail. You gladly step inside.

The interior of the cabin is a sanctuary of comfort and simplicity. A crackling fire in the stone fireplace invites you to sit and bask in its warmth. The furnishings are rustic yet inviting, with plush armchairs positioned and sturdy wooden tables.

You take a seat in an armchair, allowing the warmth from the fire to envelop you. The gentle crackle of the flames and the soothing aroma of tea, coffee and hot cocoa combine to create an atmosphere of utter relaxation. You sit back and enjoy the sounds of the forest—the chirping of birds, the whisper of the wind through the trees, and the gurgling of the nearby mountain stream.

As you sip your warm beverage, you gaze out the window at the landscape that surrounds the cabin. Countless fir trees stand proudly, each boasting its own distinctive characteristics. Some appear slender and delicate, while others are broader and more robust. You marvel that nature's creativity knows no bounds, even within a single species of tree.

Inside the cabin, you notice shelves lined with well-loved books, their spines worn from countless readings. The titles span a variety of genres, from adventure tales to philosophical works, inviting you to lose yourself in their pages during your stay. Nearby, a stack of board games and decks of cards beckon, offering the promise of lively entertainment on cozy evenings spent indoors.

In another corner of the cabin, a writing desk bathed in sunlight catches your eye. Piles of blank notebooks and pens wait patiently, inviting you to capture your thoughts and memories of days spent outdoors.

After a time, you rise from the armchair, feeling refreshed. You step back onto the porch, taking a deep breath of the fresh mountain air, feeling the sun against your skin. You embark on your descent down the mountain. The journey feels remarkably smoother compared to your arduous ascent, thanks to the restorative visit to the cabin and the gradual slope of the trail ahead.

Now it's time to leave this mountain. Come back to your present environment, bringing this feeling of peacefulness into the day or evening.

Journey 26: Aurora Borealis

Inhale slowly, counting to three, filling your lungs with air. Exhale gently, counting to three, releasing any tension. Repeat this process, taking three deep, purposeful breaths, allowing your body to relax more deeply with each one.

Imagine you are in the heart of a remote northern wilderness in the evening. It's winter and you stand in an expansive, snow-covered field, far away from major cities. The ground beneath your feet is soft, with a thick layer of freshly fallen snow that sparkles under the moon's gentle light. Snow cushions each step you take.

The landscape is dotted with tall pine trees covered in snow, creating a striking contrast to the dark night sky. The air is so cold that you see your breath, but your winter boots, insulated hat, gloves, and a thick down coat keep you quite warm.

As your eyes adjust to the darkness, the first signs of the Aurora Borealis manifest above. What starts as a faint glow on the horizon slowly intensifies. Ribbons of green light stretch across the sky, growing brighter and more vivid with each passing second. The lights dance, a gentle sway at first, then they move with increasing fervor. With a powerful green glow visible for miles, they completely illuminate the sky.

The Aurora's bright green colors give way to deep purples, vibrant pinks, and occasionally, a splash of crimson red. These hues weave together in an ever-changing view. The vivid colors appear, intertwine, move across the sky, and then disappear.

The lights cascade downward from above, forming dazzling columns of color that seem to extend from the very heavens themselves. At moments, these vibrant streams merge and separate in a dynamic dance. This movement creates a spectacle that resembles a cosmic ballet, with the lights pulsating and swirling, alive and performing.

You reach out your hand toward these ethereal lights, feeling a connection to something far greater than yourself. The lights seem to respond, swirling directly overhead, to a cascade of color that envelops everything.

As the Aurora pulses and undulates across the sky, it resembles a curtain caught in a gentle breeze. Bursting forth with a radiant display of vibrant purples, the curtain of light transitions seamlessly into a luminous green. Then, in a mesmerizing transformation, the hues shift once more, painting the sky with a soft, enchanting pink glow.

The pink hues gradually morph into shades of deep purple. Yet, just as quickly as they appeared, they fade, only to reappear in another part of the night sky. You now see a purple ribbon streaking across the sky, disappearing into the darkness.

A green light takes center stage, dancing across the sky in graceful ribbons, swirling and intertwining. With each movement, it seems to grow in intensity, culminating in a dazzling explosion of vibrant green hues that disappear. A strand of delicate pink appears high above, casting a soft glow. It then transforms into a radiant green hue, adding to the beautiful vista.

In the expansive, snow-covered wilderness, a lone fox traverses the terrain. Its vibrant red-orange fur is a stark contrast to the pristine white surroundings. With fluid and graceful movements, the fox navigates the snowy landscape with ease. It raises its head to gaze up at the spectacle unfolding in the night sky and seems transfixed by the Aurora Borealis.

As the fox resumes its journey, disappearing into the vast expanse of wilderness, its presence is a reminder of the resilience and adaptability of nature, even in the most challenging environments.

Now the sky bursts forth in a radiant display of pink light, only to fade and reappear in another part of the sky. The pink transforms to purple, then disappears. Green streamers begin their dance across the sky, swirling together and exploding in a shower of purple. A strand of pink appears high above and then changes to a green glow. A purple strand crosses the other lights and then disappears.

The Aurora Borealis continues to paint the sky. The lights create a flowing mane of a celestial horse galloping across the heavens, its vibrant trail a mixture of greens and blues. In another moment, the patterns shift, resembling a phoenix rising, its wings spread wide in a burst of purples and reds.

A distant howl of a wolf pierces the night. It's a sound that resonates with the wild beauty of this place. The call is both haunting and beautiful, a reminder of the untamed nature of the wilderness. It's far away, growing fainter over the next several minutes.

Taking a deep breath, you exhale slowly, watching as your breath forms a mist in the air. The sky above is so absorbing that you have forgotten about the cold. Despite the temperature, you feel warm with your many layers of clothing.

You walk, leaving a solitary trail of footprints in the snow. The movement keeps the cold at bay. Soft snow beneath your feet is a reminder of your connection to this incredible place. The Aurora seems to follow.

Eventually, you come to a frozen lake. The ice reflects the Aurora's magnificent display. Standing at the lake's edge, the dance of emerald greens above is reflected on the lake's frozen surface. Swiftly, the hues transition to radiant yellows that now intertwine with the green. You see these beautiful colors on the frozen lake and marvel at the beauty of this experience.

Now it's time to leave this frozen world. Come back to your present environment, feel your body, and take this sense of wonder and peacefulness into your day.

Journey 27: Rainforest

Inhale slowly, counting to three, feeling the air fill your lungs. Exhale gently, counting to three, releasing any tension. Repeat this process, taking three deep, purposeful breaths, allowing your body to relax more deeply every time you exhale.

Imagine you are in a dense, thriving rainforest, surrounded by lush foliage and towering trees. The atmosphere is thick with humidity, carrying the scent that saturates this area—a mixture of rich soil and rain-soaked greenery. A winding path unfolds through the heart of the rainforest, its soft ground a carpet of soil and fallen vegetation.

The forest canopy stretches overhead. Sunlight filters through, casting rays of light onto the ground. Plants thrive in abundance, with some growing on top of others. Towering trees, draped in vines and adorned with brightly colored flowers, reach skyward.

Among these, orchids live on the branches and trunks of trees, ranging from ghostly white blooms that seem to float among the greenery to the vivid splashes of pink, purple, and yellow. Each orchid displays its beauty distinctly. Some have slender stems and graceful petals in bright colors, while others boast thick, green leaves that frame their blooms.

One orchid catches your eye with petals the color of fiery red and orange. Each petal, edged in a delicate yellow, seems to flicker even without a breeze. The orchid's heart glows a deep, velvety red, while its slender stem offers a stark contrast to the explosion of color above. This orchid perches high on an ancient tree along the path.

Intertwined with the orchids, the passion flowers weave their way through the foliage, their vines using tendrils to grasp and ascend. The flowers feature a mesmerizing blend of colors—deep purples, striking blues, and pristine whites—with a center burst of filaments creating a surreal halo effect. Their large, star-shaped flowers stand out as a vivid contrast against the deep green colors of the rainforest.

The variety of sounds in this rainforest unveils its complexity. Exotic birds call out, weaving a chorus of melodies that reverberate among the trees. The distant hoot of an owl—'hoo hoo'—melds with the vibrant, chirping trills of a toucan, and the rhythmic tapping of a woodpecker fills the air. Each sound tells a story of life and survival.

You continue down the path to a crystal-clear stream. The deep water flows gently through dense vegetation. A school of neon tetras glides effortlessly. These small, yet vividly colored fish show a striking contrast of hues, with the front half of their bodies shining in a brilliant blue, and their tails marked by a vibrant red. Each one has a luminous blue stripe that runs the entire length of their body, beautifully paired with a vivid red stripe that begins midway and extends to the tail. Agile and swift, they dart through the water, weaving in and out with a playful energy that suggests a game of hide and seek.

You follow the path into a clearing where the bright blue sky emerges. Here, the sunlight pours down, bathing the area in a bright light. In this glade, a slight movement catches your eye. A Blue Morpho butterfly is off to your right. Its brilliant, iridescent blue wings, edged with delicate black edges, catch and reflect the light in a dazzling display of color. As you glance around, you see many more of these butterflies dancing among the trees. These majestic creatures, with wingspans reaching up to six inches across, are like living patches of sky floating through the air.

The clearing thrums with the flutter of dozens of these splendid butterflies. They have moments of activity and rest. One flutters off to land on a plant and then joins the others in their rhythmic ballet. Several seem fascinated by a small shrub, and they open and close their wings as they explore this bush. You stand still, and a butterfly lands on you. The stunning blue wings against the stark black edges are even more magnificent when viewed up close. It lingers for just a moment before taking flight to join the others.

As the afternoon unfolds, the forest light takes on a deeper, richer quality, bathing the landscape in a soft, golden light. The intense brightness of midday softens, casting gentle shadows that fall across the path.

The air quickly becomes alive with the distinctive calls of frogs, finding refuge in the damp crevices near small streams or beneath the foliage. Their sounds vary—some emit deep, resonant croaks, while others offer softer, more delicate 'ribbit' noises. Adding to this natural symphony, crickets contribute their persistent chirping, a melody created by the rhythmic rubbing of their wings. The echoing calls of frogs and the steady chirp of crickets imbue the forest with a palpable sense of life.

As you absorb the forest sounds, a frog on a nearby leaf grabs your attention. About the size of a large walnut, its skin is a vibrant tapestry of greens with speckles of blue, almost like it's wearing the forest itself. The eyes, wide and reflective, seem to take in everything. It sits still, as if contemplating its next move. In a sudden burst of energy, it leaps to another spot, disappearing into the greenery. This glimpse into the frog's life shows its remarkable adaptation to the forest, where camouflage and agility are key to survival.

Take a final deep breath, filling your lungs with the fresh, moist air, and let it out slowly, feeling a sense of peace and rejuvenation.

It's time to leave the rainforest. Come back to the present and take this feeling of wonder and peacefulness with you into your day or evening.

Journey 28: Grand Castle

Inhale slowly, counting to three, filling your lungs. Exhale gently, counting to three, releasing any tension. Repeat this process, taking three deep, purposeful breaths, allowing your body to relax more deeply with each one.

Picture yourself visiting a grand castle nestled within an ancient forest. This castle opens its doors for visitors to explore it. The air is infused with the scent of blooming wildflowers and the rich, earthy aroma of the surrounding forest that encroaches on the castle grounds.

The castle's formidable stone walls and soaring spires stretch skyward, piercing the clear, bright blue expanse above. Encircled by over 1,000 acres of pristine wilderness, the castle dominates the landscape. With approximately 30,000 square feet of living space, this regal building is home to over one hundred bedrooms, many sitting rooms, and other formal entertainment spaces.

The castle was constructed over 200 years ago. Its architecture created a residence of unparalleled beauty. The castle's expansive grounds, a combination of untamed forests and meticulously manicured gardens, are intended to impress visitors. Roses and other colorful flowers live among carefully trimmed shrubs.

You walk to the threshold of this castle where history and luxury intertwine. Passing through the ancient, weathered wooden doors, you step into the grand entrance hall, a space with high, arched ceilings. A majestic staircase spirals upward to the lofty second floor. Shafts of sunlight pierce through the ornate stained-glass windows, scattering a display of many colors across the cool stone floor. From the entrance hall, you proceed to the heart of the castle, which is the great hall on the first floor.

The great hall historically served as the center of castle life, where guests were received. It is an immense space, with a towering fireplace large enough to stand in, its hearth once a source of warmth and light for gatherings. Regal tapestries hang along the high walls, each one telling tales of valor and history, their colors rich against the stone. Plush chairs with rich and deep-colored upholstery form several sitting circles, inviting guests to sit and enjoy regal hospitality. Intricately carved wooden details on the chairs and table legs speak of the craftsmanship and artistry that went into their creation, each piece of furniture a work of art.

You now enter the dining room, designed to accommodate an impressive number of guests, with a long, grand dining table that stretches towards another immense fireplace. The table seats over fifty people. It's set with dishes and silver, ready to host a banquet. The tall ceilings vault skyward, decorated with frescoes that depict scenes of harvest, celebration, and the changing seasons. These pictures add visual stories to the room.

Further down you enter the library, where shelves, reaching towards the ornate ceiling, cradle leather-bound books and scrolls. You touch the spines of several thick books, each embossed with gold. On either side of the room, rolling ladders provide access to the highest shelves, where more volumes reside. This collection might well number over 100,000 books.

Next, you ascend to the second level and visit a guest bedroom suite. A large, antique four-poster bed sits in the center of the room. A beige silk comforter with an intricate emerald-green design sits on the bed. Heavy curtains, crafted from the same silk, frame the windows. Surrounding a marble fireplace, a seating area in luxurious emerald silk, mirrors the bed's elegance. The room's antique furnishings, including a wardrobe and a writing desk, seem ready to whisper stories of the past.

Down the hall you find the king's and queen's private apartments. The king's quarters feature a study with strategic maps and a library rich in military volumes. His bedroom has a large, canopied bed with deep burgundy coverlets and curtains.

The queen's bedroom contains light-colored blue silk draperies and hand-painted furniture. A vanity adorned with an assortment of jewels and perfumes suggests she has exquisite taste. Beyond her bedroom lies a private garden terrace, a secluded haven where she can look out over the garden and surrounding countryside.

Further down the hall, you enter the queen's large sitting room. Here, the air is fragrant with several bouquets of roses placed on side tables. The walls display a soft yellow pastel color. Sunlight filters through lace curtains to warm the space. This room feels cozy, with its plush sofas and delicate chairs in light colors. You can imagine the queen entertaining female nobility here, having tea, and discussing important matters.

Descending to the main floor, the men's rooms welcome you with their robust, earthy ambiance of wood and leather. A smoking room, furnished with sturdy armchairs and a curated selection of spirits, has its walls adorned with stags' heads and nautical maps that suggest tales of adventure. These rooms are dark, with deep green walls, adding to the warmth of the atmosphere.

After leaving this area, you step into the ballroom. This room features gilded mirrors, sparkling crystal chandeliers, and walls decorated with ancestral portraits of kings, queens, princes, and princesses. This vast hall springs to life in your imagination, filled with the echoes of past gatherings, the elegant swirl of gowns, and many dancing feet, all under the gaze of ancestors along the walls.

Now it's time to leave the castle. Come back to your present surroundings and bring this sense of wonder and peacefulness into your day or evening.

Journey 29: Moonlit Garden

Inhale slowly, counting to three, filling your lungs with air. Exhale gently, counting to three, releasing any tension. Repeat this process, taking three deep, purposeful breaths, allowing your body to relax more deeply with each one.

Imagine it is evening and you're in a moonlit garden, a place where tranquility and mysterious beauty exist after dark. Breathe in the cool night air. Above, the full moon hangs in the dark sky, accompanied by a scattering of stars. The moon's gentle light bathes everything in a serene glow.

A stone path meanders through the garden, inviting you to explore this place transformed by the evening light. As you walk, the firmness of the stone beneath your feet anchors you in the present moment. You walk slowly, drawn toward a cluster of white flowers that seem to glow in the light.

Drawing closer, you realize these enchanting blooms are moonflowers, which have the distinctive habit of unfolding their petals only as the evening arrives. They gently close them with the dawn's first light. They sway gracefully in the evening breeze, their ivory petals shimmering, inviting you to draw nearer. You extend your hand and gently touch the silky surface of a petal, marveling at its delicate softness beneath your fingertips.

As you admire the cluster of moonflowers, a delicate fragrance wafts in the air. The scent is reminiscent of vanilla laced with jasmine. As you stand there, the aroma grows more pronounced, weaving its way through the garden. You breathe in this scent, which is calming.

You proceed along the stone pathway, which leads to a secluded rose garden that takes on a mystical appearance under the moonlight. The transformation is striking. Light pink roses assume a soft, ghostly hue. Yellow roses, usually bright and cheerful by day, now shimmer with a dark, golden glow. The dark reds deepen into rich, velvety shadows. As the night breeze wanders through the garden, the roses sway gently, performing a graceful dance. This motion releases their fragrances. You admire these roses under the moonlight and breathe in the scent of these beautiful flowers.

Continuing past the rose garden, the soothing murmur of water beckons you, leading you to a secluded, circular pond. This water is a hidden jewel nestled within the garden. Surrounded by ferns and moss-covered stones, the pond's surface reflects the moon's face above.

Water lilies float with an air of serenity on the water. The dark water creates a beautiful contrast with the delicate white and pink flowers. Their stunning beauty emerges from the muddy depths below, a testament to the transformative power of growth and resilience.

A stone statue of an ancient goddess stands near the pond, wearing a flowing robe that drapes elegantly over her form. The folds of her garment, carved with great skill, suggest movement, as if she might come alive at any moment. Her face is serene, with softly carved features that radiate a sense of peace and wisdom. Her eyes gaze into the distance, pondering mysteries only she knows. A delicately chiseled wreath of flowers lies on her head, symbolizing her sovereignty over the natural world. Her flowing locks of hair cascade over her shoulders, adding to her majestic appearance.

In one hand, she holds a vessel, perhaps once overflowing with the waters of life, now serving as a home to trailing ivy that has taken root in the crevices of her stone. The other hand extends outward, as if inviting visitors to come into her garden and reflect on the beauty and tranquility of her world.

As you draw nearer, the urge to touch her stone robes becomes irresistible. As you reach out, the first sensation is the cool, unyielding surface of the stone against your skin, a stark reminder of its age and permanence. The texture varies under your fingertips. In some places, the stone is quite smooth. In other areas, it's rough, likely because of weather and the effects of time.

The goddess appears truly majestic. The moon's soft light bathes her in a gentle glow, highlighting the intricate details of her form and the calm expression on her face. In this moment, she is a timeless witness to the beauty of the night, reigning over her moonlit domain.

Coming across a quiet wooden bench, you sit down and enjoy the beautiful view. Above, the night sky is filled with stars. Suddenly, a cloud drifts in front of the moon, casting shadows across the garden. The light dims momentarily, transforming the scene. Silhouettes of the trees sway gently, their outlines softened in the dimness. The statuesque figure of the goddess changes, her features and form briefly obscured.

As the moon regains its full brightness, it illuminates the goddess statue. She seems to have come to life; her features brightened with an otherworldly radiance. A soft light bathes the surrounding garden, as if all the world has dimmed to let her shine. It's as though she stands ready to impart her ancient wisdom to those who are nearby. In this magical moment, the garden becomes her stage, and she is its centerpiece, with her timeless beauty and enigmatic presence.

It's time to leave this moonlit garden. Come back to your present environment and take this peacefulness with you into your day or evening.

Journey 30: Coral Reef

Inhale slowly, counting to three, filling your lungs with air. Exhale gently, counting to three, releasing any tension. Repeat this process, taking three deep, purposeful breaths, allowing your body to relax more deeply with each one.

Imagine you are standing on the soft, warm sand of an ocean beach, the sun warming your skin. Waves lap against the shore. You breathe in the clean air and gaze at the calm water.

After putting on your snorkeling equipment, you step into the clear, welcoming ocean. As you wade deeper, the water reaches your chest, and you swim. You can't help but smile at the sight of your large flippers. Dipping your face below the surface, the outside noise fades, replaced by the peaceful silence of the underwater world. The only sound is your breathing through the snorkel, a steady, reassuring rhythm.

Sunlight pierces the water, casting light across the sandy bottom. The seaweed beneath you moves in a swaying motion as you swim toward a coral reef. The water feels cool and invigorating against your skin, its buoyancy lifting you. You float along the surface, gazing at the ocean bottom below. You watch as a vibrant orange fish gracefully swims below you, leaving you curious about its destination.

As you draw closer to the coral reef, the bottom shifts from a sandy plain to a kaleidoscope of life and color. At the edge of the reef are branching corals, like miniature trees, in shades of green and brown, with hints of pink and blue. Fan corals stand out, waving gently in the water currents, displaying a spectrum of yellows, oranges, purples, and reds, their soft bodies adding movement to the scene. This underwater marvel stretches out before you for about one mile (1.6 kilometers).

The large, dome-shaped brain corals stand out prominently amidst the reef's bustling activity, their intricate surface patterns resembling a human brain. Dressed in rich shades of greens and browns, occasionally tinged with hints of blue, these majestic corals command attention. They serve as havens for the many fish who weave among them. Vibrant clownfish, with their unmistakable orange bodies striped in white and edged in black, dart among the coral, seeking refuge within the undulating tentacles of sea anemones. The cylindrical bodies of the sea anemones are crowned by an array of tentacles, and range in size from mere inches (a few centimeters) to over three feet (one meter). Some are red, others are orange, green, blue, and purple.

Meanwhile, graceful angelfish glide past, their majestic fins unfurling like delicate silk in the gentle current. Their elongated diamond-like bodies are adorned with many colors, from deep blues and greens to striking bright yellows, accentuated by contrasting stripes. Schools of shimmering silver fish move in unison, their bodies reflecting the light. You appreciate this wonderful scene of the diverse corals and brightly colored fish swimming around this area.

You float above the coral reef, careful not to touch it. The array of colors is captivating. In one area, the corals are green and brown, mirroring the earthy tones of a forest. Another section bursts into life with vibrant pinks and blues, reminiscent of a vivid sunset sky. You see an array of fish, each species gracefully darting through the coral's nooks and crannies. This beautiful underwater realm, teeming with life and color, unfolds before you, offering a glimpse into the complex and interconnected world of the coral reef.

Beneath you, a small sea turtle glides effortlessly, its movements unhurried. You follow at a distance, watching as it navigates the reef, stopping occasionally to feed. It doesn't seem to notice you as it goes about the business of its life.

Your journey takes you over a patch of soft coral, their surfaces waving gently in the ocean. Their flexible branches and elongated whips sway with the ebb and flow of the currents. These corals range from the fiery reds and oranges of sunsets to the soft pastels of dawn. Their tiny tentacles reach out to capture passing nutrients.

Here, hidden among the folds of the coral, you spot a small octopus, its body changing colors and textures as it moves within the coral reef. The octopus is an expert at camouflage, a creature of great intelligence and mystery.

You listen to the subtle sounds of this underwater world—the distant, gentle rumble of the ocean beyond the reef and the quiet rush of water around you. For a moment, you feel as if you never want to return to land.

As the sun begins to lower in the sky, the colors of the reef deepen, becoming even more vibrant. The changing light adds a layer of magic to the scene. The once bright greens, yellows, and blue corals take on deeper hues—emerald, gold, and sapphire.

Eventually, it's time to return to the shore, propelling yourself forward with the rhythmic kicks of your flippers. The sensation of the water rushing past you reinvigorates your senses. As you swim, your movement warms you.

Reaching the shallows, you feel the familiar tug of gravity as your feet find the sandy bottom. You peel off your mask and take a deep breath.

It's time to leave this wonderful adventure. Come back to your present environment and carry this feeling of peace and wonder into your day or evening.

Journey 31: Zen Monastery

Inhale slowly, counting to three. Exhale gently, counting to three, releasing any tension. Repeat this process, taking three deep, purposeful breaths, allowing your body to relax more deeply with each one.

Imagine yourself on a journey to a Zen monastery, a sanctuary of mindfulness and serenity, nestled deep within a mist-covered forest. The world around you slows as you walk through the woods to this retreat.

A thick blanket of mist surrounds the trees, creating an ethereal atmosphere. The path underfoot is a mosaic of smooth stones, laid down by those who have walked this way in search of peace before you. You feel each step along these smooth stones as you walk mindfully. Each stone feels slightly different, and each one connects you to the earth.

The gentle sound of a bell rings through the forest, its clear tone guiding you along the path. The sound is both inviting and profound, a call that beckons you to let go of your thoughts and simply be.

As you follow the sound, the forest slowly reveals the Zen monastery. Its wooden structure is simple, fitting in perfectly with the natural surroundings. This architecture is a testament to the Zen practice of finding beauty in simplicity.

You enter the grounds around the monastery, which are immaculate. A path winds through gardens of carefully tended plants and large stones arranged in patterns that invite contemplation.

The monks, dressed in simple orange robes, move with deliberate, graceful steps along the paths. Their presence is a reminder of the discipline and dedication to mindfulness that this place nurtures. They move in silence and yet seem fully present.

You are invited to join the monks in the meditation hall. Wooden floors and large windows connect the calm interior with the natural world. The air carries a delicate fragrance of incense. Cushions are neatly arranged on the floor. Here, the walls, painted with earthy colors and the ceiling of exposed wooden beams, create an atmosphere of rustic beauty and simplicity. The hall is spacious and open, with large windows that look out onto the misty forest, connecting you with the natural world even as you turn your gaze inward.

You select a meditation cushion and settle onto this comfortable, supportive surface. The distant, harmonious sounds of the forest drift through the open door. Birdsong and the sound of trees rustling fill the silent hall. These sensory experiences envelop you, serving as a reminder that mindfulness is a profound way to connect more deeply with the world.

The meditation begins with the ringing of a bell, its sound clear and pure, creating ripples in the silence. You focus on your breath, paying attention to each inhalation and exhalation. With each breath, you feel more grounded, more centered, more at peace. You watch your breath come and go, which is soothing.

Thoughts also come and go, like clouds in the sky, but you return again and again to your breath, to the present moment. This practice is simple yet profound, where every breath is a reminder of the richness of the present moment.

As you meditate, you realize the interconnectedness of all things—the way the mist envelops the forest, the way the trees nurture the moss, the way the monks' practice nurtures their mindfulness. You see everything is part of a vast, intricate web of life, and you, too, are part of this web, connected to the forest, to the monastery, to the monks, and to every living being.

The meditation session comes to a close with the ringing of the bell once more, its sound echoing the impermanence of all things. The bell reminds you to cherish each moment. As you slowly rise from the cushion, you are grateful for these wonderful opportunities to slow down and be mindful.

You are now invited to engage in a walking meditation within the monastery grounds. The undulating patterns in the carefully raked gravel at the heart of the Zen Garden represent the movement of water. The gravel's silvery hue glistens in the light. Scattered purposefully across this sea of gravel are islands of moss and strategically placed rocks of various sizes and shapes. These rocks, worn by time and weather, evoke a sense of permanence and stability amidst the ever-changing world.

You place one foot in front of the other and then step again and then again. Absorbed in the movement of your legs and feet, you walk slowly while traversing the garden. You feel every muscle and appreciate how much your body does for you when you move.

Surrounding this garden are paths lined with stepping stones, leading you on a mindful journey through the forest. As you walk, the deep greens of the forest foliage reveal themselves in varying shades and textures. Ferns unfold their fronds at the base of towering trees, displaying their bright green leaves. Moss clings to tree trunks and carpets the ground, its lushness a testament to the life-giving moisture of the mist.

It's time to leave the monastery. Slowly bring your awareness back to your present environment and carry the feelings of peace and tranquility into your day or evening.

Anne E. Beall, PhD

Anne E. Beall is an award-winning author whose books have been featured in *People Magazine, Chicago Tribune, Toronto Sun, Hers Magazine, Ms. Career Girl*, and she's been interviewed by NBC, NPR, and WGN.

Her book, *Cinderella Didn't Live Happily Ever After: The Hidden Messages in Fairy Tales* won a Gold award from Literary Titan. Her sequel book, *Only Prince Charming Gets to Break the Rules: Gender and Rule Violation in Fairy Tales and Life* won a Silver award from Literary Titan.

She has published in several literary journals, including *Minerva Rising Press, The Raven's Perch*, and *Grande Dame Literary Journal*.

She received her PhD in social psychology from Yale University and is the founder of the strategic market-research firm, Beall Research.

Every day, she engages in meditation and firmly believes in the power of quiet introspection, no matter how it is practiced.

Acknowledgements

I want to thank several people who made this book possible. The first person is Michael Tuck, my husband, who encouraged me in this endeavor. He has been tremendously supportive of my many writing projects and is always happy to entertain my next idea.

The next person I'd like to thank is Danielle Sunshine, who edited an early version of this volume and whose suggested changes made these chapters better from a sensory perspective. She also took clunky sentences and transformed them into more appealing prose. She was a great pleasure to work with throughout this project.

I would also like to thank Judi Lee Goshen, who read the book in its entirety and provided great edits for the final version. She is a great friend and an inspirational writer.

And thank you, reader, for purchasing and reading or listening to this book. You are the reason that I write every day.